A Soft Landing
after a
Bumpy Ride

- -

MAKING FRIENDS
WITH THE INNER LIFE

Charles E. Ortloff

WESTBOW
P R E S S®
A DIVISION OF THOMAS NELSON
& ZONDERVAN

WestBow Press books may be ordered through booksellers or by contacting:

WestBow Press
A Division of Thomas Nelson & Zondervan
1663 Liberty Drive
Bloomington, IN 47403
www.westbowpress.com
844-714-3454

All Scripture quotations are taken from the New Revised Standard Version Updated Edition. Copyright © 2021 National Council of Churches of Christ in the United States of America. Used by permission. All rights reserved worldwide.

ISBN: 979-8-3850-0440-9 (sc)
ISBN: 979-8-3850-0441-6 (e)

Library of Congress Control Number: 2023914234

Print information available on the last page.

WestBow Press rev. date: 08/10/2023

THE INTRODUCTION

The Origin of this Book

Every morning at dawn, I wandered through the forest,
With absolutely no idea where I was going in life.
And then, one morning the path appeared.

On May 20, 2020, I was diagnosed with stage 4 cancer.

Seven months before this, I retired. I had served as a pastor for 42 years. I enjoyed my work but I was tired, ready for something else. But what? I drifted along in my journey assuming that I had plenty of time to figure things out.

But then, my drifting came to an abrupt end. As my wife and I sat in the doctors' consultation room, I received the answer to my question of "what's next?" I had cancer. I was stunned and at a loss for words. The doctors spoke at length about treatment plans but there was no mention of any cure. I was grateful for all the wisdom and experience they brought to my care plans. I don't remember much of what they said, with the exception of one thing: "We will try to keep you alive for as long as possible so that you die of something else." I had never heard of a treatment plan like this. It got my attention. This was serious.

While the doctors spoke to me about their plans for my life, my mind drifted off into a tangle of thoughts about my own plans. I immediately realized that the few markers I did have for retirement were gone. In their place, I was given a path I didn't want to take, a destination I didn't want to consider. I felt numb. I didn't know where to begin this journey with cancer. I didn't know what to say – to my wife, to the doctors, or to God.

As I left the consultation room, I finally thought of a response to all that my oncologist had told me. I asked, "Should I be planning my funeral?" That probably wasn't the most thoughtful response but it was where my heart was. He gently patted my shoulder and looked at me with compassion. But he said nothing. That was my answer. He didn't know how quickly the cancer would run its course. I could see no soft landing in my future.

When I left the consultation room, I wanted to think about something else, anything else, even for a few moments. But I couldn't get cancer out of my mind. I wanted to return to my old life. But I was walking through a desert in a windstorm. When I looked back at the sand to see where I had been, my footprints were gone. There was no path back to those endless possibilities of retirement. A voice in my head kept repeating: "This is really happening to you. You have stage 4 cancer." I felt alone and hopeless.

The next morning, I couldn't get out of bed. The reality of the diagnosis was spiraling deeper and deeper into my heart. It felt like an elephant was sitting on my chest. After a while, something inside of me said, "Get up. Go for your walk." Having no better plan, I got up and took my usual walk in the forest that morning. And the next morning. And the next morning. As weeks turned into months, every morning at dawn, I wandered through the forest, with absolutely no idea where I was going in life. And then, one morning the path appeared.

Now three years later, I still have cancer. There is still no talk of a cure. But I am learning to reimagine my life. It all begins with early morning walks before dawn where I have long conversations with my inner life. I walk each morning until I am ready to face the day.

On a physical level, with my medical team, I'm working very hard to be healthy. But on an inner level, I am not fighting cancer. I am welcoming cancer as an honored guest who brings me one gift after another.

And now, I have once again found a direction for my life. People notice how I'm reacting to this diagnosis of cancer. "You seem to be doing well," is the usual comment I hear. I am surprised that people seek out my advice, maybe even more so now than when I was a pastor. The diagnosis of cancer provides me with a new, and maybe better, platform for "walking with people."

Now after three years, I am beginning to see a path ahead of me. The first step or two seem clear now, the rest of the journey remains shrouded in a cloud of uncertainty. For now, I find comfort not in having control over my journey but in having the companionship of the inner life for the journey. The "40 Days of Conversation Starters" in this book summarize my morning conversations with my inner life.

Making Friends with the Inner Life

What exactly do I mean by "making friends with our inner life?" Some might call the inner life our heart, mind, or soul; or, maybe our conscience or our intuition; or, even our muse. Maybe it is all of the above.

I have chosen the words, "inner life," to direct our attention to what often goes unnoticed. There is a truth right here inside of all of us. This truth becomes apparent to us as we pay attention to the circumstances of our lives, our hopes and dreams, our mistakes and frustrations, and especially the wisdom we have gathered along the way from those who have gone before us. We only need encouragement to unlock it. I am called to help people process the wisdom inside of all of us.

To make friends with the inner life is like taking a weeklong road trip. Imagine that we have riders in the backseat of our car, but we pretend that they aren't there. This makes for a stressful trip. One of our passengers may be car sick. Another passenger may know the roads we travel better than we do. Another passenger may be a good friend. Though we try to ignore the passengers, we can sense conversations in the backseat, maybe even arguments, maybe illness and sadness. Ignoring all this is not helpful. Far better to pay attention to what is going on in the backseat. So it is with our inner life. There is alot going on, but by nature we pretend it isn't there. In my three years with stage 4 cancer, I have learned that making friends with my inner life is the key to finding that soft landing after a bumpy ride. This is what I share in this book.

The Structure of the Inner Life

I have observed that my inner life includes four ongoing interactions, moving in a spiral going deeper and deeper into my inner life until I come to God and my soft landing:

Our thoughts, emotions, body sensations, and wants
And then deeper into
Our life stories, including those bumpy rides and soft landings
And then deeper into
Our three inner voices: separated self, connected self and the watcher
And finally, at the very center,
We find God, who is our "soft landing"

My first encounters with my inner life were with my thoughts, my emotions, my body sensations and my wants. I paid attention to my sadness, my fears, my anxiety, my questions, my doubts, that ache in my stomach, my wants for my life. And in doing so, I felt my heart's burden lighten, just a little.

In time, I noticed my life story. I processed what had happened and what may happen next. I had important conversations with myself: How do I prepare my family and my friends for my death? What legacy can I leave my family and my world?

Then, as I continued to go deeper into the inner life, I noticed not just one inner voice but three. I call these the **separated self**, **the connected self**, and **the watcher.**[1] The "40 Conversation Starters" are designed to help us become aware of these three voices and then to bring their conversations to a healthy resolution.

Finally, as I spent time with these first three components of my inner life, I quite naturally and easily moved into a conversation with God. Suddenly, I had all sorts of things to say to God. And I was eager to hear what God had to say to me through the Bible, nature, friends, and my life experiences.

The Structure of the Conversation Starters

Through these Conversation Starters I do not give many answers to life's journey. Instead, I encourage all of us to pay attention to our own journey and to know truth not only on an intellectual level but also on an experiential level. To be able to say, "This is my truth," is a very powerful thing. May these Conversation Starters peak our interest into going just a little deeper into the wisdom of our own inner life.

---

[1] For a more complete description of the three voices, see Appendix I,

Each day I break down the conversation starter into four parts: observations, stories, practices, and finally, some last thoughts.

Observations

We begin our time of looking within by considering observations about the topic for the day. When looking at our lives, it is easy to mindlessly see things as we've always seen them. When this happens, we may miss the wisdom offered to us in the circumstances of our lives, a wisdom we so desperately need for our journey today into uncharted territory. I invite you to look at life with beginner's eyes. See the circumstances and events of life as if for the first time.

Stories

Stories can inform and motivate us. They can direct and comfort us. Stories are the poetry of life, the depth and breadth of life. Stories are important. The stories I tell are true. Some have a historical authenticity about them, others may feel more like the parables from the Bible. But as one elder put it, "I don't know if the details happened this way, but I know that the story is true." The stories I share are true.

Practices

After we have seen life a little differently, we are ready to live life a little differently. If this were a class in school, it wouldn't be a lecture, it would be a lab. This is the time to discover our own truth. We need to be careful of merely adding more words to our notebooks. Better to take a few words to heart each day and put them into practice than to fill up more notebooks only to put them on the shelf to gather dust.

Some Last Thoughts

As a way of summarizing our discussion for each day, we consider one thought and one quote to carry with us as we go about our day. We return to these, again and again throughout the day, letting them inform the unfolding circumstances of our lives today.

How to Use the Book

The title of this book, "Finding a Soft Landing after a Bumpy Ride," comes from my experience of a soft landing after a bumpy plane ride. We've probably all had those rides when the plane is experiencing more than just a little turbulence. Flying can have this rhythm of bumpy rides and then, hopefully, soft landings. That's how flying is. That's how life is, too. Times of turbulence and then soft landings, again and again.

Cancer is my bumpy ride. We all have our bumps along the way. For some people, like me, it may be some life threatening illness. For others, it may be the long goodbye we face when a loved one is dying. Or, our bumpy ride may involve challenges in our relationships or jobs; money issues and the economy; homelessness, hunger, social issues and politics; or war and rumors of war. The list is endless. I invite you to take a look at your own life. What are the things that worry you or that keep you up at night? Can you name just one bump in your ride right now?

Some of our bumps along the way are not too bad, we easily ride them out. But others may be the "humpty dumpty" bumps where it seems that nothing can put our broken lives back together again. Hold on to your own unique "bump" as you work your way through these forty days of conversation starters with your inner life.

Once you have in mind your own bumpy ride, we are ready to travel together with this book. How should you read it? However you read it is the best way. Maybe you read it from cover to cover in one reading. Maybe you read one "Day" a week. Maybe you read one "Day" each day for 40 days as I imagined it might be read. Maybe you read it by yourself as part of your own practice of prayer, meditation, or personal growth. Maybe you read it with family members or in a small group together with other fellow travelers. Whatever makes sense to you is a good place to start our time together in these "40 Days."

As you process and apply the forty days to your life, you will discover how to have productive conversations with the voices of your own inner life. It may take you several readings of this book to become comfortable with this process. But once you begin paying attention to your inner life, you will find your own wisdom that will guide you when you walk and comfort you when you rest. There will be a calm that flows from deep within you.

One Last Thought

As I wrote this book, I tried to imagine you. I wondered, "What bumps along the way are you experiencing? How might I help you travel towards a soft landing?" In answering my own questions, I have found it helpful to remember the people I have served as a pastor for 42 years. So much of what I share in this book, I have shared with many dear friends along the way. These are my thoughts and practices that were still cooking on the back burner of my heart and mind when I retired. I am grateful for the encouragement of many friends to write this book.

I especially have written for my family and for my friends new and old. I think especially of the little ones. You all mean so much to me. For those who join me on this 40 day journey, this is my legacy to you.

We're all just walking each other home.
— Ram Dass

CONTENTS

Day 1   Those Inner Voices....................................1

Day 2   Be the Watcher 4

Day 3   Hiding in Plain Sight 7

Day 4   Of Cages and Keys....................................10

Day 5   An Early Morning Walk, The Joy of God's
        Presence 13

Day 6   Partners and Co-Creators with God.....................16

Day 7   Muscle Memory..19

Day 8   Scarcity 22

Day 9   A Good Life and A Good Ending 25

Day 10 Humiliations..28

Day 11 The Great Trees in the Forest.........................31

Day 12 Breathe...34

Day 13 God is Everywhere and in Everything 37

Day 14 Forgive Life...40

Day 15 A Work in Progress.......................................43

Day 16 The Hero's Journey 46

Day 17 Surrender with Love 50

Day 18 Relationships are More Important than Rules..........52

Day 19 The Issues are in the Tissues...........................55

Day 20 Be Present 58

Day 21 Save Us From the Time of Trial 61

Day 22 Dare to Be Vulnerable...................................65

Day 23 What to Do with the Troubling Stuff?.................68

Day 24 What to Do with the Pleasant Stuff?...................72

Day 25   Gratitude..75

Day 26   Remember the Poor..................................78

Day 27   Holding a Baby 81

Day 28   Choose the Life We Have 84

Day 29   Laughter..87

Day 30   Be Our Own Easter..................................90

Day 31   Walking into the Light.............................93

Day 32   Decluttering..96

Day 33   Imagination...99

Day 34   The Ten Black Beans 103

Day 35   Amazing Love: The Contemplative Path............... 107

Day 36   Saved and Safe...110

Day 37   After the Crisis...113

Day 38   Expectations...117

Day 39   Welcome Our Separated Self.................. 120

Day 40   God's Last Word 123

DAY 1

....

Those Inner Voices

Make friends with the inner life,
Find that soft landing after a bumpy ride.

Introduction

We all have conversations with ourselves. As we prepare for an important meeting, we rehearse what we will say. As we take off on a weeklong road trip, we wonder if we locked the front door. Today, we consider our conversations with three inner voices.

Some Observations to Ponder

The inner life is that place where we process the outer circumstances of our lives, consider how we feel and think about these matters, and ultimately, how we shall then live. The inner life is our control center. In the words of Galatians 2:20, — "It is no longer I who live but Christ who lives in me," — I find a brief but succinct description of the three inner voices that I discovered in my long walks each morning after my diagnosis with cancer.

The first voice is that of **the separated self**. I believe Paul refers to this voice with the words: "It is no longer I who live." This is an earlier voice of scarcity and fear that need not influence us, but it still does, in so many ways.

The second voice is that of **the connected self**. I believe that Paul speaks of this voice with the words: "Christ who lives in me." This is our new self born of Christ, alive in Christ, the voice of compassion and abundance.

Finally, the third voice is that of **the watcher**. I believe that Paul speaks of this voice with the words "in me." This is the one who stands behind the other two voices, the one who chooses which of the first two voices to follow. This is you and I.

The Stories that Shape Us

Jesus began his public ministry with 40 days in the wilderness (Matthew 4:1-11). There in the wilderness, I notice the same three inner voices that I found in my own daily walks at dawn. The devil seems to be the voice of the separated self, a voice of scarcity and fear. He encourages Jesus to feed himself by turning stones into bread. He also tells Jesus to save himself from the cross by just worshiping the devil. This separated self framed Jesus' life in a way that would keep Jesus small, separated from God and the world, and afraid, unable to fulfill his calling.

Jesus seems to balance the arguments of the separated self with the wisdom of what I describe as his connected self. He quoted from his "go to" list of favorite Scripture passages. He reminded his separated self of God's promises to take care of him, to provide for all his needs. The connected self framed Jesus' life in a way that opened him up to face the challenges of his life with hope and optimism.

Finally, I see the watcher appear. Having heard the voices of the separated self and the connected self, Jesus made his choice to live the life that was a soft landing. He would not live a life of fear and scarcity but of compassion and abundance. Rehearsal was finished. He was ready for what awaited him.

For the rest of his life, early each morning, Jesus went off by himself to pray. There are many answers to the question, "What did Jesus do during his time of prayer?" I believe Jesus revisited that conversation he had with the three inner voices there during 40 days in the desert. Each morning, he might have posed the same question he posed in the wilderness: "Which voice will I follow today, the one of fear and scarcity or the one of compassion and abundance?" After answering this question, he would be ready to face his day.

A Few Practices to Consider

First, memorize Paul's summary of the inner life from Galatians 2:20: "It is no longer I who live but Christ who lives in me." Notice how each of the three voices is defined. Return to this passage each of our 40 days together.

Secondly, understand that these three voices are a simple path into the inner life. As we engage with them, we can engage more deeply with God, and ultimately find our soft landing.

Finally, start to pay attention to each of the three distinct voices. See how they enter into a conversation with each other about the circumstances of our lives. This conversation is the key to moving beyond a bumpy ride and finding that soft landing.

Some Last Thoughts

It is a gift to know the contrasting voices of our separated self and our connected self and then to make a decision about how we shall live.

Which voice will you follow today?

DAY 2

··

Be the Watcher

Most people I know are overly identified
with their own thoughts and feelings.
They don't really have feelings; their feelings have them.
— Richard Rohr

Introduction

Today we focus especially on being the watcher, standing back just a little from all the noise in our lives, and especially those conversations between the first two voices.

Some Observations to Ponder

There needs to be some space between the watcher and the other voices. Without this space, we can be taken captive by powerful thoughts or emotions.

To become aware of ourselves as the watcher, we must understand that there is such a voice in our inner life, and that voice is our voice. We need some quiet time, some intentionality, some practice in stepping back from life and our knee jerk responses to life.

The Stories that Shape Us

I vividly remember that day, May 20, 2020, in the consultation room of the oncology department. My doctor got right to the point. "The tests are back. You have stage 4 cancer." I remember immediately pulling back from that news. I was aware of my doctor's words. He told me that they would try to keep me alive. His voice was the voice of my connected self. He offered me a hope that for the moment was hidden from me in that fog of cancer.

I was also quite aware of what my separated self was up to. I sensed all of his possible knee jerk responses to this diagnosis: I could fall apart in tears, or cry out in anger, or blame someone for this mess I was in. I was aware of what the separated self was up to. But it wasn't me. I didn't need to react or respond, I just quietly watched.

I vividly remember this drawing back from both conversations — with my doctor and with my separated self. I was present in the same way I might watch a movie. This was not a conscious choice on my part. It just happened. I remember being surprised by my calm, detached response to the news of cancer. It was pure grace. I didn't understand yet the role of the three voices of my inner life, but I did experience them. This wasn't my soft landing, not yet. This was only the first step that in time would get me there.

A Few Practices to Try

When we begin to lose ourselves in our opinions or strong emotions, slowly repeat these words, as often as necessary:

> I have emotions but I am not my emotions.
> I have thoughts but I am not my thoughts.
> I have wants but I am not my wants.
> I have dreams but I am not my dreams.
> I have a body but I am not my body.

Begin to notice that presence, that consciousness, standing just a little apart from the highs and the lows of life. Begin to notice yourself. Be the watcher.

Some Last Thoughts

Practice being the "watcher." For a moment, set aside your thoughts or emotions. Be completely neutral. No expectations. Just watch to see what is happening.

> Be the silent watcher of your thoughts and behavior.
> You are the stillness beneath the mental noise.
> You are the love and joy beneath the pain.
> — Eckhart Tolle

DAY 3

Hiding in Plain Sight

There are many paths to God. I have chosen
a simple path – a child's path.
Paying attention to my life, I discover
"God hiding in plain sight."

Introduction

For decades I have traveled down many paths seeking God but
with limited success. Now in the second half of my life, I have
chosen a different path, a simpler path, a child's path. I have chosen
to find God in the ordinary events, people, and circumstances of
my life. I have chosen to find God hidden in plain sight.

Some Observations to Ponder

For many people, God is far away and difficult to find. To find
this distant God, some take the path of reading many books,
trying to understand God. Others take the path of self sacrifice,
trying to be like God. And still others take the path of spiritual
highs and ecstasy, trying to experience the glory of God. I have
chosen a different path, a child's path – to find God hiding in
plain sight.

I see my chosen path has many similarities to Jesus' path. In
his teaching, Jesus directed our attention to life: families who

are struggling, a farmer who plants wheat and discovers weeds, shepherds who love sheep that stray, and common things like water, wine, and bread. In his life, Jesus met people where they were: at weddings and funerals, chance meetings along the road, dinners and parties, even in people's bickering. One thing seems certain: wherever you are, Jesus is there. In fact, those are the very last words we hear from Jesus' lips in Matthew's gospel: "Remember, I am with you always," (Matthew 28:20).

The Stories that Shape Us

Sarah was a soft spoken, kind woman in her mid sixties. She was a wife, mother, grandmother, a retired pharmacist, she sang in the choir — an ordinary person.

Sarah was admitted to the hospital for emergency surgery. She had a potentially life threatening illness. As doctors and nurses tended her they noticed something special about Sarah. Though all about her were working at a hurried pace, she was that calm in the eye of the storm. After leaving her room, the staff commented to one another, "There seems to be a glow about Sarah."

When we were alone, I asked her about this, "You seem to be doing very well with all this." In her humble way of not wanting to draw attention to herself, she thought for a moment and then simply said, "I guess I am." She paused again, as if trying to find the right words. Finally, looking out the window, she said in a soft voice, almost to herself, "I love to garden. After years alone out in my garden, I can sense God with me there. That's nice." She paused again, as if wondering how much more to say to me, if anything. Then she turned to me, gently smiled and whispered as if it were some secret, "God is here, too." Her smile broadened. She would say no more about it. I would have to figure the rest out for myself.

A Few Practices to Consider

Stand back a little from life. Be the watcher. Note the events of life. Observe feelings and thoughts connected to the circumstances of life. Take time with this. Be gentle. Don't force any idea or feeling. Just let things come on their own.

Don't critique life. Instead, be present to it, like a grandma delighting in her grandchild taking her first steps. Imagine God right next to us, gently gazing upon our life.

Listen carefully for God's still small voice. Watch for any calm, joy, compassion or understanding. That could be God. What might God be saying to us? What would we want to say to God?

Some Last Thoughts

Sometimes I think God is playing a game of "hide and seek" with us. It can be a challenge to find God. So we stop looking, but don't stop. Keep an eye out for "God sightings." They are everywhere.

There is nothing I can say to you to explain divine love.
Yet all creation cannot seem to stop talking about it.

— Rumi

DAY 4

Of Cages and Keys

The small man builds cages for everyone he knows.
While the sage ... keeps dropping keys all night long
For the beautiful, rowdy prisoners.
— Hafiz

Introduction

Today, we talk about cages and keys. One is the domain of our separated self, the other is the domain of our connected self. Watching for those cages and keys is an easy way to become conscious of which voice is on stage right now.

Some Observations to Ponder

The inner life may seem quite confusing, hard to get our minds wrapped around it. But really, it's as simple as noting the two voices: the separated self spins small stories of fear and scarcity, we feel that we are in a cage; the connected self tells this grand story of abundance and compassion, we are given the key that sets us free from all those self imposed prisons. Know which voice is on stage at all times.

The Stories that Shape Us

One day, Mary and Martha, two sisters, had guests drop in for a meal — Jesus and his disciples (Luke 10:38-42). Martha busied herself with preparations for the meal. Mary did not. She just sat and listened to Jesus. This bothered Martha. She approached Jesus, demanding that he tell Mary to help make the meal. Jesus sided with Mary not Martha. Mary made the right choice. Jesus' response surprised Martha, probably it surprised Jesus' friends, too. Maybe it surprises us. We think, "How can Mary's choice be the right one?"

If all we are thinking about here is our next meal, then it's hard not to side with Martha. For Martha, there seems to be an inner conversation going on. "We've got guests that need to be fed. Why doesn't Mary help me? Why is Mary being so selfish?"

This is the separated self speaking and building several cages: one cage for Martha who identified completely with her own anger, another cage for Mary who felt Martha's hurt directed at her, and even a cage for Jesus, who experienced Martha's anger directed at him. The separated self made cages for them all.

What if Martha had seen this situation differently? Instead of making the next meal her top priority, maybe the more important thing was to listen to Jesus' comforting words. What if Martha could have reframed her situation? What if she had thought, "How many times do I have Jesus right here in my own living room teaching us? This is really an extraordinary event! We can eat later. We should listen now."

That's the voice of the connected self: the key to unlocking all the cages the separated self had built. Martha could free herself from being a victim. Mary could be freed from the separation with her sister. And Jesus could be freed from Martha's anger. The connected self holds the key for all three cages.

A Few Practices to Try

Our separated self is so sneaky. It has many ways to trick us into being afraid. Its schemes are as endlessly evolving as this year's flu virus. Carefully note how the separated self comes into our life today.

The voice of our connected self is weak. It isn't Christ or God who is weak. But rather, it is our communication link with God that is weak. It can often have a lot of static or be so soft that we don't notice it. Or, we just forget to make time for this communication. We need to pay attention to it and give it our encouragement throughout the day.

How do we strengthen the Christ voice in our lives? Think about the Bible and all that we have learned from it. Think about creation as a reflection of God's loving presence. Think about the songs and poetry and stories that make our hearts glad. Think about what gives joy, hope, peace, compassion and all the rest. Take good care of the connected self today.

Some Last Thoughts

As little babies are comforted by being wrapped tightly in a blanket, so too, we are comforted when wrapped tightly in the hope and love of our connected self.

My separated self builds cages for everyone he meets.
My connected self keeps dropping keys all through the night
For the beautiful and rowdy prisoners.
– A Paraphrase of Hafiz

DAY 5

An Early Morning Walk,
The Joy of God's Presence

These mountains you are carrying,
You were only supposed to climb them.
– Najwa Zebian

Introduction

There is a tight connection between heart, mind, and body. Health in one of the three can influence the other two. Walking is such a good way to experience physical health.

Some Observations to Ponder

I love this conversation starter about walking. As I read what others have said about walking, apparently others do, too.

> "An early-morning walk is a blessing for the whole day," – Henry David Thoreau.

> "All truly great thoughts are conceived by walking," – Friedrich Nietzsche.

> "If you are in a bad mood, go for a walk. If you are still in a bad mood, go for another walk." – Hippocrates.

> "When a man moves away from nature his heart becomes hard." – Lakota.

A 30-minute walk each day improves cardiac health, reduces excess body fat, prevents weight gain, strengthens bones. Walking reduces the risk for cancer or type 2 diabetes. You develop a healthy attitude about life by walking. Walking is completely free.

And as you walk, maybe instead of carrying those mountains of fear and worry, with Christ you can climb them, get to the other side of them. And be done with them.

The Stories that Shape Us

Prior to my diagnosis of cancer, I started every day with a walk outside. My early morning walks were a special time, a holy time. The morning after I received the diagnosis of stage 4 cancer, I had a hard time getting out of bed. Cancer weighed heavily on my heart. I just laid there thinking to myself, "It's not a dream. You really do have cancer!"

Then I heard that quiet voice of the connected self, "Get up. Go for your walk." So I did. There in my early morning walks, I had the conversations we are sharing together through these 40 Days of Conversation Starters. Many times, especially at the beginning, I didn't know what to think about this cancer business or what to say to God. So I just walked. At worst, even when nothing seemed to be happening, I took some joy from the endorphins of walking and a little sense of accomplishment for having walked for an hour. I did feel a little better just from walking.

But almost every morning, as I got near the end of my walk, I felt better about my life. Nothing had changed except I felt more connected to myself and my situation in life. And it was okay.

God's presence seemed a little more real to me. I found hope to make it through the day.

The next morning I would start all over again, pouring out this jumble of feelings and thoughts: the incredibly painful fears of the separated self and the just as incredible promises of the connected self pointing me to God's compassion and presence. These were challenging conversations with my separated self and my connected self. But once I got it all out, I was ready for one more day. Each day got just a little better. Just a little.

A Few Practices to Try

Walk just a little more each day. Observe your feelings. Check how you are doing in a week, a month, a year. Ask friends for any observations they might have about you. Be prepared to hear good news.

Watch the close connection between our mind, heart and body. Keeping our body healthy with daily walks also provides healing for our mind and heart.

Some Last Thoughts

Instead of carrying those mountains of fear and worry, with God's help we can climb them. And then, getting to the other side of them, we can be done with them. Finally.

> "Adopt the pace of nature: her secret is
> patience." – Ralph Waldo Emerson.

DAY 6

....

Partners and Co-Creators with God

Love is the constant act of revising and
retelling your own story in real time.
You don't do it by yourself. You do it with someone else.
– Bruce Feiler

Introduction

We are not alone in life. Each day, together with God, we write a new chapter.

Some Observations to Ponder:

There comes a time in life when we realize that we can't go it alone. We desperately need people in our lives to help us write the next chapter. We are stuck. We've come to the end of our own wisdom and bright ideas. We are open to advice.

But even the advice of others, as comforting and helpful as it may be, sooner or later also comes to an end. That's when we turn to God with great earnestness. We are open to the possibility of being partners with God in writing our next chapter.

The Stories that Shape Us

"Lord, what shall we do today?" was the question I had posed with God for several years before retirement. As I did so, my life got so much easier. I no longer was swimming upstream but going with the flow.

This was true in my work. I no longer proposed ideas for the church to follow and then worked hard to get people to agree to do them and then worked even harder to get these ideas accomplished. Instead, the congregation and I watched and waited to see what God was doing, then we just joined God. Together, we co-created our next chapter. Easy.

I did the same co-creating in my personal life. I had been doing a lot of writing. As I walked each morning, I opened myself up to whatever God wanted me to write. And each morning, like that "manna" for the children of Israel in the desert (Exodus 16), God provided me with all the ideas I needed for my writing that day. I learned to co-create with God in all of my writing. Easy.

So then, when I received my diagnosis of cancer, I had a practice to fall back upon. I went out into my own desert each morning, having absolutely no idea what would happen next. I just waited for God to show up. And God did. But this time things weren't as easy.

This path has been painful for my separated self, it has done a lot of grieving over loss of control. But after three years, I'm beginning to understand this new chapter of my life. Cancer is my new platform to walk with others: a challenge for my separated self, a joy for my connected self.

A Few Practices to Consider:

To write a new chapter in our story every day, begin with the prayer, "Lord, what shall we do today?" And at the end of the day, consider how that went, how well we paid attention to God's directions, and how surprised we are by God's grace and love.

Doing this in little things, everyday things, prepares us for that "humpty dumpty" bump in the road when our life is in pieces and no one knows how to put it back together again. We know the drill. We know the question to ask, "Lord, what shall we do today?" We lean into our day waiting for God to show up, even in the bumpiest of rides.

Some Last Thoughts

Change does not come easily for our separated self. We can expect a lot of grief from it. Change for our connected self is a wonderful by-product of a daily walk with God. Easy.

Today, with God as our partner,
We write the next chapter of our lives.

DAY 7

....

Muscle Memory

Practice what you know.
It will help to make clear
What now you do not know.
— Rembrandt

Introduction

When our mind can't imagine the way ahead, we trust our muscle memory.

Some Observations to Ponder:

It isn't just our brain that has memory, our muscles do, too. We are good at some pretty complex activities that require little or no conscious thinking like playing golf or the piano, or even driving a car.

Consider Jesus' time with his friends, he was always teaching them, building muscle memory. He sent them out on a missionary journey, and they returned surprised by how well things went. He took them out into a storm, that time they were a little less successful in learning the lesson to remember and find comfort in Jesus' constant presence, but later they would remember. He told them to feed 5,000 hungry people, again, they didn't do well at the time. But all this together built up their muscle memory needed for when they were on their own, but really they were never on their own. That too would become part of their muscle memory.

The Stories that Shape Us

At the 2016 Rio Olympics, runners Abbey D'Agostino (USA) and Nikki Hamblin (New Zealand) competed in the women's 5,000-meter event. During the race, somewhere around 3,200 meters, the two runners collide, bringing them both to the ground. D'Agostino noticed Hamblin was hurt and needed help.

Later, Hamblin told the press, "When I went down it was like, 'what's happening? Why am I on the ground?' And suddenly there's this hand on my shoulder, like 'get up, get up, we have to finish this!' I'm so grateful for Abbey for doing that for me. That girl is the Olympic spirit right there."

Both girls eventually made it to the finish line. Hamblin came in second to last and D'Agostino came in last with her twisted ankle. Their good sportsmanship got them into the finals. The news headlines read: "What a beautiful race!" A race to remember.

How did that moment of compassion happen? Having trained her whole life for this one race, how did Abbey D'Agostine assess the situation, ponder her options and make a decision to stop and help? All in a split second? Her muscle memory was so strong it decisively silenced any thoughts from her separated self about winning the race. She was in a class of Olympic champions all by herself.

A Few Practices to Try:

Think of Christ as our coach or teacher.

When we have a coach, we are given things to do that will make us better athletes. When we have an instructor for our cello, we are given special scales and etudes to play. All to help us become better musicians.

So the question for us today is "Who really is our coach?" Our separated self who only wants what it wants, inviting us to live a rather self centered life? Or, our connected self who is coaching us to live compassionate lives, inviting us to become more like Christ?

Watch carefully to see what muscle memory we are building up today. Work with your true coach.

Some Last Thoughts

So much of life is "practice, practice, practice." See everything in life, from the smallest detail, to the most impactful of events, as practice. Learning to lean into God and become more like God.

> If you want others to be happy, practice compassion.
> If you want to be happy, practice compassion.
> — Dalai Lama

DAY 8

Scarcity

Strive first for the kingdom of God and his righteousness,
And all these things will be given to you as well.
Matthew 6:33

Introduction

Scarcity is at the heart of the separated self's message to us. Whenever we think about scarcity, we can be certain that the separated self is "on stage" in our life.

Some Observations to Ponder:

Consider the news about the trouble in our world, nation, or community. The stories differ dramatically in their details. But if we peel back the onion far enough, there is just one story being told by the separated self, again and again, a story of fear and scarcity.

Scarcity drives our consumer culture: the need for more and more. Scarcity drives nations to war, individuals to lie and cheat and steal and hurt others. Scarcity keeps us from sharing with those in need, there may not be enough for us and for them. We learn to listen to this voice very early in life, a dominant voice of our culture.

The Stories that Shape Us

In all four stories about Jesus in the Bible, the miracle of feeding of the 5,000 appears in each. Few stories have that place of honor, not even Jesus' birth. The feeding of the 5,000 is an important story about scarcity and about letting go of our separated self.

Large crowds had gathered about Jesus. They came to be healed. Jesus had compassion for them. All day long he walked among them, healing them. The disciples were concerned about how all these people would be fed. They thought Jesus should send the people away. But Jesus turned the question back to them, asking, "Where are we to buy bread for these people to eat?" (John 6:6). This shocked the disciples. They had next to nothing to share, just a couple of fish and a few loaves of bread. They experienced scarcity. Jesus maneuvered them into a place of scarcity. How odd.

Jesus waits a moment for this moment of scarcity to sink in. Then he directed the people to sit down. He took the five loaves and two fish, blessed them, broke them, and gave them to the disciples. They fed the whole crowd. And after all had eaten, the disciples picked up 12 baskets full of food. It was a miracle of abundance.

In every telling of the disciples' earliest memories of their time with Jesus, this story was told. In our moments of scarcity, Christ stands with us, providing all that we need.

A Few Practices to Try:

Learn to be the watcher. See how the separated self uses scarcity to frighten us. See how many different ways the separated self comes at us. How tricky the separated self is. It's always the same thing, but it comes with a different twist.

Note also that voice of the connected self. In Philippians 4:5-6, Paul writes, "The Lord is near. Do not worry about anything." How seriously do we take that promise? Imagine Jesus sitting in the car with us or walking down the path with us. Do we really need to have any fears?

Again, the connected self speaks to us in Matthew 6:33, "Strive first for the kingdom of God and his righteousness, and all these things (i.e., food, drink, and clothing, the basics) will be given to you as well." This can be a challenge for some. Maybe Jesus isn't asking us to stop paying any attention to the basics of food and drink and clothing. Maybe it is a matter of "putting the cart before the horse." Put the inner life and the kingdom of God first, and the outer life comes along just fine.

Having carefully listened to each voice, decide which voice to follow. In the evening, ponder, "How did it go?" How we process this determines to what extent we can find a soft landing even in the midst of a bumpy ride.

Some Last Thoughts

Watch carefully how our lives unfold. How quick we are to go to a place of scarcity. Slow this process down. Wait. Remember God's promises and faithfulness from the past. Are these challenging moments opportunities for us to live into abundance?

The Lord is near. Do not be anxious about anything.
Philippians 4:5-6

DAY 9

....

A Good Life and A Good Ending

Goodbyes are only for those who love with their eyes.
Because for those who love with heart and soul
There is no such thing as separation.
— Rumi

Introduction

We all want a good life and also a good death. They are connected.

Some Observations to Ponder:

So then, "What is a good ending to our life?" Our separated self
tells us: "There is nothing good in death, no soft landing as life is
stolen from us." Identifying with the separated self, we fear death.

We've probably all seen the bumper sticker that reads: "Whoever
has the most toys at the end, wins." Really? After a while, most
of us realize that the point of life may be more than accumulating
things. Then what is the point of life? Our answer to that question
about life gives clarity to our questions about death.

How we live life and how we die are directly connected by a
golden thread. It is our friendship with God that makes life so
sweet and worth living now. And it is the same in death, our
friendship with God is everything. Nothing changes as death

nears. Nothing to fear. What we have now with Christ, continues, and only gets better and better.

The Stories that Shape Us

Mary's father was a pastor. She loved her father, a kind man who took good care of her. He taught her about our calling to become like Christ. She took that teaching to heart. She lovingly took up the practice of being more like Christ each day, more in love with Christ and life, each day.

I knew Mary for over a decade. I remember one occasion when she came into my office and asked for advice. She at times would lend money to a casual acquaintance. This person was taking advantage of her generosity. She asked me, "Should I continue?" I said, "Maybe you've done enough." She thought about that for a moment. And then, replied, "No, I've got the money. I can help. I think that's what Christ would do." On that day, I thought to myself, "I'm living in the voice of my separated self. Mary's living in the voice of her connected self. That Mary! She understands the inner life far better than I do."

Mary faced her own death with this same optimism and joy. She had a few months to prepare. Of course, she would have rather lived longer with her husband. But when it became obvious that would not be the case, she shifted her attention to what was coming. "Oh, I can't wait to see Mom and Dad again! I wonder about those mansions in heaven that Dad always talked about." And then she smiled. She lived her last days encouraging us to imitate Christ in all things. She was more in love with God and life each day, even her last day.

A Few Practices to Try:

Let this be our practice and our goal, in life and in death:

> To be more in love with God today than yesterday,
> And to be more in love tomorrow than today.

What an intriguing plan for living: not in scarcity but abundance. This is living well and this is dying well. But how do we do this?

Think of those sweet moments from the past with God. A quiet walk, conversations at dawn or before bed. Helping someone in need. Loving a little child. Can we do more of that? Think of what we have seen in others. How do they enter into that sweet daily dance with God? What can we learn from them?

Spend some quality time with God, our dear friend, building that loving relationship. See what happens. Live well. Die well.

Some Last Thoughts

We are called to live into this delicious friendship with Christ. "To be more in love with Christ today than yesterday, and to be more in love tomorrow than today."

> Heaven all the way to heaven.
> – St. Catherine of Siena

DAY 10

Humiliations

Pulling out the chair beneath your mind
And watching you fall upon God.
What else is there for Hafiz to do
That is any fun in this world!
– Hafiz

Introduction

How do we deal with all the humiliations of life? There are so many.

Some Observations to Ponder:

When we think about it, life is just one humiliation after another. As a child, we feel singled out when we make a mistake in school. As a youth, we want to fit in with the cool kids, but rarely do. At work, a place built on accomplishments, humiliations can end a promising career. As we age, we need help with physical things that were once private matters, and we forget even the simplest of things.

Humiliations are part of life, an essential part of our inner journey.

The Stories that Shape Us

Simon Peter was one of Jesus' closest friends. But he had a lot of rough edges that needed to be smoothed off before he could be of much use to God. All the disciples had rough edges, but Peter's moments of humiliation often take center stage in the story of Jesus' life.

When Jesus announced that he must go to Jerusalem to die, Peter stood in his way forbidding Jesus (Matthew 16:23). He acted as if he was smarter than the master. Jesus sharply scolded Peter. On the evening before his death, Jesus warned all the disciples that they would desert him that night. Again, Peter corrected Jesus, they will desert you but I never will. Jesus told Peter that not only would he desert Jesus, he would also deny Jesus three times (Matthew 26:33-35). That night, in the courtyard of the high priest, Peter did just that, as Jesus said he would (Matthew 26:69-75). After Jesus' resurrection on Easter, Peter felt completely humiliated. He had talked a good game, but in the end, he was a failure as a friend of Jesus.

Here's the interesting thing. Not only does Jesus forgive Peter, but he welcomes Peter back as if all this needed to happen (John 21:15-19). It seems counterintuitive to us. Richard Rohr, in his book by the same title, calls it "Falling Upward." It's not just that some bad behaviors need to be gotten rid of, but we need a complete change of heart. This can only happen by falling off that pedestal of self-pride and that self-made life that our separated self has built for us. We need to fall before we can enter this upward path to God. This falling is a great shame for the separated self. But for the connected self it is a great joy. Learn to embrace humiliations, the path to transformation.

A Few Practices to Try:

First, notice how we have responded to humiliations in the past. Did we try to hide from them? Did we try to ignore them? Or, did we beat up on ourselves? Or, get angry with others? Or, did we process them?

Secondly, right now, today, watch for humiliations. Embrace at least one humiliation today. Welcome that humiliation. Smile. See it as a gift. Our separated self will fight this all the way. But remember, we are not our separated self.

Finally, as we stay fully present to this humiliation, notice how it drives us into the loving arms of God. Our separated self can't tolerate a loser! But our connected self offers us the loving arms of Christ to catch us.

Some Last Thoughts

In our humiliations, we face the separated self's worst fears. Our connected self knows there is no other way to fall into the loving arms of Christ and find that soft landing.

Facing life's humiliations,
Our separated self cries,
Our connected self laughs.

DAY 11

The Great Trees in the Forest

Stand still, the trees ahead of you and the
bushes beside you are not lost.
Wherever you are is called here. The
forest knows where you are.
You must let it find you.
– David Wagoner

Introduction

My father loved his time in the forest and gave me his legacy of
joy. Like the great cathedrals of Europe, the forest is a holy place
for me, a place of wonder and mystery and God.

Some Observations to Ponder:

There are two parts to every forest. The undergrowth and the
canopy. The undergrowth is all the messy stuff of a forest jumbled
together in this survival of the fittest: grass, bushes, and small
trees, and also the dying and the dead bushes and trees. The
canopy is all the great trees, way up there, together they blend into
an umbrella of security over all the life below, quietly keeping
watch over everything.

The Stories that Shape Us

At the top of every great tree in the forest, the view is the same.

The first few weeks after my diagnosis with cancer, my walks in the forest changed. I walked even more slowly. I focused on the dead and decaying trees on the ground. I saw myself in these. Then, one day, I stopped in a place along the path where four great Norway pines created a box. That day, lost in my usual musing, I was suddenly awakened by a great wind blowing through the top of the four Norway pines. It was magnificent, powerful, and fearful all at once, silencing all the chatter of my separated self.

In that strong wind blowing above me and all around me, I suddenly saw my life differently. My life wasn't just the dead and dying of the undergrowth. My life was the whole undergrowth: the young trees, the beautiful plants, the not so beautiful buckthorn weeds, and even the dying trees; and my life was also that wonderful canopy of love embracing it all, the good and the bad. In an instant, I saw that everything belonged: my mistakes, my poor judgments, my cancer, and even my death. As these great trees watch over everything with a sturdy tenderness, in every season, and in all the storms of life, so too, God watches over me, warts and all.

I came back again and again to these four great Norway pines that now had become "my prayer chapel." There my heart opened up to God and life as I pondered the view from the top of the great trees in the forest. Under that great umbrella of oaks, elms, and pine trees, I understood that I lived in a similar umbrella of God's love, through all the seasons of my life. I breathed in deeply and smiled knowing that I was taken care of by that same sturdy tenderness.

I wrote this Haiku poem. I love to recite it as I enter the forest.

Stand of Norway Pines
Softly rustling in the breeze
Smiling, I look up.

A Few Practices to Try

As we walk through a forest, our eyes first turn to the undergrowth with all of its messiness. We see everything from a dualistic point of view. We like some things, and we dislike other things; we label some things good and others bad. We often do the same with our view of the world, other people, and even our own lives. We label our world and ourselves: good and bad. This is the separated self's view, a dualistic view.

When we look at the canopy way up above us, we are challenged to see it in the same way that we see the undergrowth. Instead of the sharp, dualistic focus of the separated self, we tend to gaze at the canopy, with soft eyes, not noticing the parts, but taking in the whole. Instead of comparing one tree against another, we tend to experience the whole canopy, the wonder and joy of being under this umbrella of protection and care. It is like walking into a grand cathedral in Europe and looking upwards.

Some Last Thoughts

As we walk through a forest, our separated self sees everything with a dualistic lens, some things are good, others aren't. Our connected self sees everything from the top of the great trees, the canopy, with non-dualistic eyes. Everything belongs and is loved.

In the religion of Love
There are no believers and unbelievers,
Love embraces all.
— Rumi

33

DAY 12

Breathe

Tension is who you think you should
be. Relaxation is who you are.
— Chinese Proverb

Introduction

Notice how breathing, especially deep breathing, is a topic for discussion in many areas of life: religion and spirituality, sports and exercise, even learning to fall asleep. Today, let's consider the spiritual practice of deep, mindful breathing as it relates to our discussion about the three inner voices.

Some Observations to Ponder

We all breathe, every day, all day. Even babies do it. What's there to practice? There is a breathing that enlivens the body, and one that enlivens the inner life.

There is this marvelous connection between our minds, our hearts, and our bodies. Our minds can teach our hearts and bodies to focus. Our hearts can calm our minds and bodies. Our bodies by deep breathing break the cycle of ruminating over our past life, or worrying about our future. We can break the spell our separated self has cast upon us.

The Stories that Shape Us

Remember a time as a child when we were angry or upset. A parent or teacher might have told us, "Stop! Count to ten!" We obeyed and it worked. By the time we got to ten, the anger had subsided, even just a little. We were no longer in the deep grip of strong emotions, but we could now stand back just a little and observe our life, and even take some advice from others.

In this childhood experience of counting to ten, we see the three inner voices. The separated self had totally taken control of our lives. We were quite unconscious of this change. There wasn't an "us" and the anger. We were the anger. But as we counted to ten, the grip of the separated self lessened. We were able to create just a little distance, we could catch our breath and become the watcher. And then we could hear that soft voice of our connected self. It was all there. As little children we experienced this truth for ourselves.

In a similar way, now as adults, deep breathing breaks the hold of the separated self, creates space for the watcher to come on stage, and finally lets the connected self speak.

A Few Practices to Try

Practice deep breathing for a minute. Take six deep breaths. Inhale through the nose for five seconds. Exhale through the mouth for five seconds. Deep breathing helps us relax our body, our mind, and our heart.

Some Last Thoughts

Practice deep breathing at the beginning and ending of each day. Practice deep breathing when feeling off balance, when momentarily lost.

> Feelings come and go like clouds in a windy sky.
> Conscious breathing is my anchor.
> – Thich Nhat Hanh

DAY 13

God is Everywhere
and in Everything

God comes to us in many ways,
Even in the things we don't like,
And in the circumstances we don't want.

Introduction

We see our lives in dualities. Some things are good, some things
are bad. We even do this with God. Sometimes God seems close
to us, other times not so much. This seeing life in dualities is
a source of great fear and keeps us from experiencing a soft
landing.

Some Observations to Ponder:

Notice the fundamental different point of view of our two voices.
The separated self sees life in dualities: everything is either good
or bad. The separated self comments about life, critiques and
compares events. It's never really happy.

The connected self sees life as a unity: God is everywhere and in
everything. There is a calm, joy, even a hopefulness. We know
that even if we can't understand life, God does, and God has this
great plan for us. Relax and enjoy the ride

Seeing God in everything is the soft landing after a bumpy ride. There is no place left from which the separated self can pop out and scare us. Life becomes a little less bad, and in time, a lot less bad, until, like a child wrapped safely in her mother's arms, all we know is love. This is our journey through our bumpy rides to our soft landing.

The Stories that Shape Us

In John's gospel, we read that Jesus is the "way," (John 14:6). Traditionally, Christians have often understood this as the path to "being saved" when we die. But I believe it can also be understood as the path to "being safe" right now.

In Jesus' death we see the "way" he saw God in the conversations of his separated self and connected self. The first word Jesus spoke from the cross was from the connected self. He prayed for his enemies who were murdering him. "Father, forgive them," (Luke 23:34). He saw God even in the tortures of the cross and in his death. If God was in these things, then God is in everything.

But as his hours on the cross wore on, he weakened in mind and body, the separated self made one last appearance with his message of fear and scarcity. Jesus cried out, "My God, my God, why have you forsaken me?" (Matthew 27:46). For that moment, he seemed to have lost this sense of God's loving presence. Perfect as he was, he was human. He identified with that separated self's voice who saw life in dualities, good and bad, life and death, God's presence and God's absence. For a moment, all he could see was the separated self's view of death.

But later, before he died, he chose once again to live in his connected self, to see all of life as this unity. God was present in every situation. So, while all about him, wherever he looked, there was only loss and defeat, he chose to see God. With his last words on the cross he confirmed God's presence even in death. "Father, into your hands I commend my spirit," (Luke 23:46). The key to a soft landing and the ending of all our fears is to learn to see the world from the perspective of our connected self, to see God everywhere and in everything. We have nothing to fear. We have that soft landing.

A Few Practices to Try:

To see God in everything is quite challenging, especially at first. Begin by watching the little things of life that you want to label as "bad." Wait. Don't be so quick to label them. Watch and see how God might be in this thing you thought to be bad. Do this with just one thing today. Watch to see if God shows up. Isn't that the storyline of Good Friday and Easter? How surprised Jesus' friends were with Easter.

Some Last Thoughts

See God in beauty and in ugliness, in truth and in lies.
See God in success and in failure, in health and in sickness.
See God in life and in death, at Bethlehem and at Calvary.

> Everyday is a good day and some
> days are even better.

DAY 14

Forgive Life

In spite of everything, I shall rise again.
I will take up my pencil which I have forsaken,
In my great discouragement,
And I will go on with my drawing.
— Vincent Van Gogh

Introduction

We're all aware of the need to forgive others, but what does it mean to forgive life?

Some Observations to Ponder:

We know about the need for forgiveness with other people. But it's maybe a stretch for us to consider that we also need to forgive life. Without giving it much thought, we may have entered into a *quid pro quo* with life. We did this, now life should do that. But life let us down. We need to forgive life for not doing its part.

What do we do with our frustrations when life has let us down? We can live with a slow, simmering anger that is always there. We can withdraw from life, lose our passion for living. We can live in **BEV** (a.k.a., **B**itterness, **E**ntitlement, or being a **V**ictim). All these responses keep us from going very deep into the inner life, keep us from experiencing our soft landing.

The Stories that Shape Us

In John's Gospel, the last chapter, we read about several occasions where Jesus met with his friends after his resurrection on Easter. On one of these occasions, Jesus publicly forgave and reinstated Peter for his words the night Jesus died. After this moment of forgiveness, Jesus told Peter that his life would be very challenging. He would be led by others to a place he didn't want to go. Jesus spoke of his death at the hands of others.

Peter had some misgivings about this. Understandable. He had expectations about life, a long life, not in any way shortened. He might have gotten angry with life, or become bitter. It was important for Peter to see this was not life letting him down. This was his calling from Christ.

He could forgive life for all its shortcomings. Life was not his soft landing. Christ was. In the end he would joyfully follow the path his friend and master had taken. Tradition tells us that, like Jesus, Peter would die by crucifixion. Peter asked to be put on the cross upside down. He thought that he didn't deserve to die as his master had died. Not the words of a bitter man but of a humble servant.

A Few Practices to Try:

Why not start today: offer our hand to life. Forgive life for not living up to our dreams and expectations. Where will we begin? We can only do this by moving away from the chatter of the separated self, and talk about "my rights!" We need to fully enter into our connected self's abundant love. There is both clarity and strength there. This is the only way to connect to our inner life and regain our passion for life.

Some Last Thoughts

We want life to save us and to make us feel safe. It won't happen. Let go and let God. Fall into those loving arms of God, experience the soft landing we desire.

Let God, not life, be your soft landing.

DAY 15

A Work in Progress

Our vision is so limited we can hardly imagine a love
That does not show itself in protection from suffering....
The love of God did not protect His own Son....
He will not necessarily protect us –
Not from anything it takes to make us like His Son.
A lot of hammering and chiseling and purifying by fire
will have to go into the process.
— Elisabeth Elliot

Introduction

Today, we consider the idea that we are a work in progress. This is such a freeing perspective for seeing ourselves and for seeing others, a place of compassion. A wonderful place to cut ourselves some slack.

Some Observations to Ponder:

In Jesus' story, his friends come off poorly, it's embarrassing to watch. They fight about who is the greatest, they argue with Jesus as if they knew better than Jesus. What hubris! When Jesus is dying, they are in hiding, afraid they might be next. You might think to yourself, "Well, they didn't know any better."

So then, what about us? We know better. We know God's plan, at least, we know that plan as it is revealed to us in Jesus' story. And yet, knowing all this, we come off badly, too. We're just like Jesus' friends. We beat up on ourselves. Where is the compassion for ourselves?

For all of Jesus' friends, then and now, it's not about learning information. It's about "knocking off the rough edges," and there are so many of them! All of Jesus' friends are being molded into Christ's image.

The Stories that Shape Us

Prior to my diagnosis of cancer, people described me as serious. They were right. Then, along came cancer. I was pushed into the deepest of all serious considerations: my own death. Life got extremely serious!

And then, I didn't die. At least, I haven't yet. I realize that now when I do die, I've had time to think about it, prepare myself and my loved ones. This was a turning point for me. I had spent my whole life climbing up this mountain called "life is really serious." Then one day, I had gotten to the top of that mountain and now I am coming down on the other side. "Weeee!" I'm running down the other side of the mountain with a sense of being carefree for the first time in my life. Life and death are no longer snipping at my heels, hounding me every step of the way. With Paul, I can say that for me to live is Christ and to die is gain, (Philippians 1:21). This is an experiential truth for me. I own it.

There's this wonderful song with the words, "How can I keep from singing?" It's about knowing that the Lord is with us in all seasons of life. I feel that way now, more so than ever. How can I keep from singing and humming? How can I keep from laughing and making jokes? I go to bed at night chuckling to myself, life is so good, I can't wait to see what God and I do tomorrow.

What is particularly enjoyable now is being open about my failings. Having faced my fears about death, fears of my shortcomings being found out by others seem so trivial. I'm so happy to be here in God's workshop. I am that soft clay in the hands of the master potter.

A Few Practices to Try:

First of all, let us remember, again and again, every day: we are a work in progress. We will always be a work in progress. To our dying day, we will be a work in progress. Hold that thought.

Then, let's "cut ourselves some slack." Lighten up when we mess up, as we will. Embrace our foolishness. Smile, have a good laugh at ourselves.

Finally, work with God today and co-create our new life in Christ.

Some Last Thoughts

Let the master continue to mold and shape our life, like the clump of clay we really are. Relax. We are in good hands. Enjoy the journey today.

> The truth will set you free but not
> until it is finished with you.
> – David Foster Wallace

DAY 16

....

The Hero's Journey

The hero's journey begins the moment we
hear Christ whisper, "Follow me!"
– Matthew 4:19.

Introduction

Today, we consider the hero's journey: doing great things in our corner of the world. We consider the stories that have encouraged us along the path of our own hero's journey. Do we have any stories that touch our heart, give us courage or hope, stories that need to be told again and again?

Some Observations to Ponder:

I have always loved stories about heroes, even as a boy. These stories framed my outer life as a hero's journey. Stories about heroes have provided me with just the right companions for my journey.

The idea of a hero's journey for all of us may seem a bit fanciful, too much the thinking of a child, not really in touch with the everyday stuff of going to work, driving kids to piano lessons, or filling out our income taxes. But consider Christ's invitation to become like him. There is much in common between being a hero and becoming more like Christ: our call to follow, the journey that is an adventure, the need for help along the way, the life changing story that we are in. Following Christ is our hero's journey.

The Stories that Shape Us

The Old Testament character Job appears to be more of a victim than a hero. He doesn't have answers. But he does have his own experience of truth: one who has been there and has come out on the other side transformed.

Job entertained the frightening thought: Does God care about me at all? In the depths of our suffering, have we not felt the same? For the bulk of Job's story, we read of friends who gave him easy answers. But they were no help. This too we've experienced. Try as we might, we can't rationalize or think our way out of some of our most desperate troubles.

What Job needed were friends who would just walk with him. Keep him on the journey. Job needed their hope to carry him when he had no hope of his own. Though Job did not find this for himself, he can be that friend for us. He knows how distant God can feel to us. He knows how annoying it is to want some answers but there are none. We need to walk THROUGH our darkest and scariest valleys.

In the same way, we might see Jesus as our hero: abandoned by God, forsaken by wisdom he cries out on the cross ("my God, my God, why?" – Matthew 27:46), given easy answers from those "friends" who gather round him at the cross ("If you are the Son of God, come down from the cross." – Matthew 27:40), and in time he came out on the other side transformed (e.g., the Easter greeting of Christians since the earliest days: "Christ is risen, he is risen, indeed!").

Job is our friend and hero, Jesus too. And after we get to the other side of our sufferings, we can be heroes for others on their journeys.

<blockquote>
When someone is broken,
Don't try to fix them...you can't.
When someone is hurting,
Don't try to take away their pain...you can't.
Instead, love them by walking beside them in the hurt...you can!
Because what some people need is to
simply know they aren't alone.
— Kelly's Treehouse, Carmen Munoz
</blockquote>

A Few Practices to Try:

Stories can be the hero's friend, a place of companionship and wisdom. As we read about heroes, we find a useful roadmap for our call to be like Christ.

When faced with a life we didn't choose, there is Mary, the mother of Jesus. Imagine the things Mary might tell us about her unexpected and unwanted journey. In that imagined conversation, what questions might we want to ask her?

When faced with impossible challenges as a youth, there is David and Goliath. Imagine what David was thinking when he decided to go up against Goliath. Where did he find the courage to face that giant?

When experiencing great wonder, there is John resting on the breast of Jesus. John identifies as the disciple whom the Lord loved. Imagine what it would be like to be so emotionally close to Jesus. His was the contemplative life, seeing the wonders of God everywhere. Imagine what advice might he give us for our own journey of deep friendship with God.

Some Last Thoughts

In the stories of the heroes who have gone before us, God gives us just the right companions for our journey: Mary when our journey is unexpected, Job when we are hopelessly alone, John when we are filled with wonder and awe.

> Who knows? Have patience. Go
> where you must go, and hope!
> — Gandalf, "The Lord of the Rings"

DAY 17

···

Surrender with Love

Mary treasured all these words and pondered them in her heart.
Luke 2:20

Introduction

Today, let us consider the importance of surrender. Not a mindless surrender of, "Well, whatever!" But a conscious surrender to God's will in our life. Surrender with love.

Some Observations to Ponder:

Life doesn't always work out the way we've planned. Then, what do we do? We can spend hours, days, years, kicking and screaming about our life. And after all that, then what? What good has our resisting life done for us? The problem remains.

The Stories that Shape Us

A soon to be mother of her firstborn child, ponders, "How will I do this? The interruptions of my sleep to feed this little one, the dirty diapers, the crying, the daily 24/7 putting the needs of this little one before my own wants and my own needs. What have I gotten myself into? I have no choice now, I'm in this!"

Then the child is born. The child is placed in the new mother's arms, so fragile, so beautiful. The child captures the mother's heart. She now surrenders but not from any coercion but out of love. She is now a mother.

> I loved you from the very start.
> You stole my breath, embraced my heart.
> Our life together has just begun.
> You're part of me, my little one.

A Few Practices to Try:

Many people have surrendered to life. They have waved the white flag in defeat. The joy and the passion are all gone. Now they just march in place. Why not "get over" the little drama our separated self has written for our life? Why not embrace God's grand story of meaning, safety, and all the rest?

But to do this, we need to surrender with love.

Some Last Thoughts

We are called to not just surrender, but to surrender with love. This is the story of Mary, the mother of Jesus. When Jesus was born, like so many other mothers, before and after her, this beautiful little baby captured her heart. She surrendered with love.

> To surrender as a victim, we remain unconscious.
> To surrender with love is the noble journey –
> Moving from the separated self to the connected self.

DAY 18

....

Relationships are More Important than Rules

You can either practice being
right, or practice being kind.
− Anne Lamont

Introduction

For many, our first introduction to religion and spirituality
was all about rules. When we were children and we broke the
rules, our parents weren't pleased with us. We concluded that
God was not pleased with us either. Rules may have taken on
a greater importance than relationships. Today, we consider
the place of our relationship with God, over against the rules
of God.

Some Observations to Ponder:

Consider the differences between children and adults, how each
engages life and God. Children find life and God in the inner life
of stories, relationships, and imagination. Adults tend to find life
and God in their outer lives of history, rules, and reason—where
God may be just a little less wonderful, a little less mysterious, a
little less God.

Leaving childhood, we've left so much behind in what makes for a rich relationship with God, such things as our imaginations and our love of stories. Jesus invites us to rediscover our inner life, that place of relationships.

Consider the stories Jesus told and the stories we tell about Jesus' life, they are really about relationships not rules: the prodigal son, the thief on the cross, or sharing a meal with sinners.

Our outer life is a bumpy ride. We may see a God of rules who is mad at us. But in our inner life we can experience a God of relationships, who is the soft landing we seek.

The Stories that Shape Us

If I had only one story with which to travel through life, it would be the story of the prodigal son (Luke 15:11-32). Everything we need for a soft landing is in this story. (If you haven't read it for sometime, read it again now. It really is a masterpiece.)

When the family is torn apart by the younger son who runs away from home, we are reminded that we are all a "work in progress" and that real transformation happens best when we are in relationships. When the prodigal son "comes to his senses," we are reminded of the importance of paying attention to our inner life. When the prodigal son is graciously welcomed into the banquet while the older son refuses to come in, we are reminded that heaven starts right now, and so does hell.

The main point of the story is this: relationships are more important than rules. We picture the father deeply saddened by his son's absence, living in that far off country. Then, seeing his son return, he makes a fool of himself. The old man runs to greet his son. He will take no chances that the son will change his mind. All is well. His son was dead and now is alive. The rules are all forgotten. The son has returned.

In the story, the older son is the voice of the separated self. He's all about rules. He wants to punish his brother. The father is the voice of the connected self. He's all about relationships. He wants to love both sons. The story does not tell us the ending. What happens to this family? Does the voice of the separated self keep the painful drama going? Or, does the voice of the connected self as seen in the father heal all wounds?

A Few Practices to Try

Consider a favorite story from the Bible. Jesus with the children? The Prodigal Son? Jesus calms the storm? Psalm 23? The Nativity? Easter? Read the story. Imagine being in the story, one of the characters. What comfort, compassion, hope, joy, guidance do you experience?

Become a child again: live into stories, relationships, and imagination.

Some Last Thoughts

The way to return to relationships at the center of our inner life and relationship with God is to return to the stories that we love, from the Bible and from other sources. Place ourselves in these stories. Experience God for us and with us.

> Your relationship with God is more important
> to God than any of God's own rules.

DAY 19

....

The Issues are in the Tissues

I listen with love to my body's messages.
— Louise Hay

There is more wisdom in your body than
in your deepest philosophies.
— Friedrich Nietzche

Introduction

There is a simple wisdom that connects the aches in our body
with the circumstances of our lives. Today, we consider the place
of our bodies in our spiritual journeys.

Some Observations to Ponder:

Take a long, gentle look at our bodies. We say someone is a
"pain in the neck." We note that we can't "stomach" what is
happening to us. We try to sleep but our problems give us no
peace. When we experience loss of a loved one, we have a broken
heart. Conventional wisdom points us to our bodies if we would
see what's going on in our inner life. What are they saying to us
in our aches and pains? Consider the possibility that our bodies
carry the pain of the separated self.

We can fool our mind, but we can't fool our body. Our mind blames others, distracts us, or minimizes issues. But the body remembers and suffers.

The Stories that Shape Us

A few years after I started work as a pastor, I came down with a serious case of pneumonia. I was laid up for several weeks and it was a couple of months before I got back to full strength. I had a lot of time to think.

I know that there are these things called viruses and bacteria. And there are things we can do to keep us from getting sick and help us get better when we are sick. I'm grateful for science and modern medicine.

I also know that I seem to be more susceptible to viruses and bacteria when "it is NOT well with my soul." When I came down with that case of pneumonia, I had been struggling in my inner life for many weeks. I was working longer and longer hours but frustrated by a lack of success. I dragged myself out of bed each morning, forced my body and mind not to do great things, but just to do anything. They tried. But they also gave me warning signals like the red lights on the dashboard of my car. I had headaches, more frequently and more severe. I had less energy to exercise. But I paid no attention to these. So, I believe, my inner life played a part in my body giving into pneumonia or how serious my illness was. In this illness of my body, I finally paid attention to the illness in my inner life.

There in bed for two weeks, I had time to think, pay attention to my inner life. I'm a very slow learner. My body needed to give me more feedback in the years ahead, even now in retirement. But, even way back then, I started to see my body as a source of truth.

A Few Practices to Try:

Notice the many ways we distract our bodies, dismissing their message to us with food, drink, work, exercise, shopping, watching TV. The list is long.

How might we make friends with our bodies when they are suffering? When our head hurts, ask, "What thoughts are overwhelming for me right now?" When our stomach aches, ask, "What emotions are bothering me today?" When we wake up at 2 am, ask, "What have I not paid attention to today?"

Some Last Thoughts

We can fool our mind, but we can't fool our bodies. The body carries the suffering we don't want to face. What suffering are we carrying now in our bodies? Is there some message our bodies have for us? Make friends with our bodies. Be gentle.

Like a good friend, our bodies hold onto our issues
Until we can face them. Are we ready now?

DAY 20

Be Present

The secret of health for both mind and body
is not to mourn for the past,
not to worry about the future,
nor to anticipate troubles,
but to live in the present moment
wisely and earnestly.
— *Buddha*

Introduction

Today, we consider the importance of being present to this time
and this place.

Some Observations to Ponder:

Being present, fully present to this place, this moment, is
challenging. Our separated self wants us to focus on the past —
reliving our mistakes or being hurt again and again by others.
Our separated self wants us to focus on the future — imagining
all that can go wrong. Scaring us again and again. Keeping this
drama going is the way the separated self is enlivened. God wants
no part in keeping these dramas from the past or future going.
They aren't helpful. God wants to meet us in the present, in the
current challenges.

It is said that in heaven, there is no past and no future. Only the present. If we would begin to taste heaven right now, we need to learn to be in the present. Go to the past or to the future only for short visits. Be present to where you are now. This is where God is.

The Stories that Shape Us

Moses was keeping the flock of his father-in-law Jethro, the priest of Midian; he led his flock beyond the wilderness, and came to Horeb, the mountain of God. There the angel of the Lord appeared to him in a flame of fire out of a bush; he looked, and the bush was blazing, yet it was not consumed. Then Moses said, 'I must turn aside and look at this great sight, and see why the bush is not burned up.' When the Lord saw that he had turned aside to see, God called to him out of the bush, 'Moses, Moses!' And he said, 'Here I am.' Then he said, 'Come no closer! Remove the sandals from your feet, for the place on which you are standing is holy ground,' (Exodus 3:1-5).

The story of Moses and the burning bush is a familiar story, even for our children in Sunday school. We emphasize the uniqueness of that experience for Moses, but not for us. It was a grace, a gift, from God. The angel of the Lord did all the work. Moses just looked. Well, maybe. Elizabeth Barrett Browning suggests a different understanding of that story.

> Earth's crammed with heaven,
> And every common bush afire with God,
> But only he who sees takes off his shoes;
> The rest sit round and pluck blackberries.
> — Elizabeth Barrett Browning

Her poem invites us to consider the possibility that every common bush is "afire" with God. If we would only be present, stop our busy lives and note what is there. God is there, in every bush, in everything.

We are in such a hurry. Going. Going. Always going somewhere. And going from here to there takes time. We can't stop and see what is right in front of us. Add to this our preoccupation with cell phones, and all the latest internet apps on the computer that grab and hold our attention, we just can't be where we are right now.

And the more we do this—hurry—the better we get at doing this—missing life, beauty, a flower, a sunset, our children growing up. The more we do this, the more we miss those things God might be trying to tell us, as Moses had experienced. Instead of "taking off our shoes" for this holy space, we just "sit around and pluck blackberries."

A Few Practices to Try:

Mindful breathing can be a good way to stay in the present. Breathe in God's loving presence, breathe out the separated self's chatter.

Be the watcher of that bump in the road. Do not be so quick to pray for it to leave. Wait and see. How does this bump cause us to be here and now? And what do we experience? Maybe a burning bush?

Some Last Thoughts

Deep breathing can be our body's way of helping us stay present. See how it keeps our attention in the present, here and now. What is our burning bush today? What surprises does God hold for us in this burning bush?

> Stress is caused by being here but wanting to be there.
> — Eckhart Tolle

DAY 21

Save Us From the Time of Trial

We impoverish God in our minds
When we say there must be answers
To our prayers on the material plane.
The biggest answers to our prayers
Are in the realm of the unseen.
— Oswald Chambers

Introduction

In the Lord's Prayer we ask God to save us from the time of trial. That's what we are doing with these 40 days of conversation. We're looking for that soft landing after a bumpy ride. Today, let's consider the prayers we offer to God to save us.

Some Observations to Ponder:

As children, prayer was one of our first spiritual practices. Our world was awfully big and scary. We prayed for God to watch over us. But some problems didn't go away no matter how much we prayed. So, many of us gave up on God, outwardly leaving organized religion, or inwardly expecting little from God.

But then, sooner or later, life gets impossible again and we give prayer a second chance, or third chance, or fourth chance. And once again, we may discover that God doesn't always save us. We keep recycling through this drama: we face a bumpy ride, we know what we need, we ask God for help, but God's help can often seem sporadic and unpredictable. We don't feel that we can count on God to help us, at least to do things our way.

Is there another way of framing this dilemma? Maybe we are posing the wrong question. Rather than asking, "Why has God let me down?" Maybe we need to ask, "Who is stunned by God's seeming inaction? Our separated self or our connected self?"

The Stories that Shape

Today, we have another story about those two sisters, Mary and Martha (John 11:1-44). This story includes their brother Lazarus. These siblings were dear friends of Jesus. Lazarus was near death. The sisters sent word to Jesus. They knew that Jesus had the power to heal their brother. They had no doubt in their minds that Jesus would heal Lazarus.

When Jesus heard that Lararus' was ill, he stayed where he was for two more days. Then he went to see his friends. By the time he arrived Lazarus had died. The sisters were grieving. When Jesus met them, they were both stunned, they asked, where were you?

Jesus then went to the tomb where they had placed Lararus' body. He told them to open the tomb, probably a cave on the side of a hill. Then Jesus shouted for Lazarus to come out. And he did. Jesus returned their brother to the two sisters. The story leaves us with more questions than answers. If Jesus could bring Lazarus back to life, and if he would do it anyway, why wait so long? Why put the sisters through all this? One answer is in our understanding of the three inner voices.

It is the separated self who grieves that day. The separated self isn't evil, it doesn't need to be punished. It is just small, inadequate – separated. The two sisters, like us, needed to let go of the drama of the separated self. This means grieving a life we had imagined. Only then, can we move on to the connected self, trusting in the relationship with God. Before Jesus brought Lazarus back to life, he taught the two sisters to look to their own connected self, trust God's promises even when the circumstances of life do not turn out the way we had hoped. There is our soft landing, even in the death of a loved one.

A Few Practices to Try:

Once again, return to the ongoing conversation between our two voices: Notice how our separated self is constantly in fear of losing the things of the outer world: health, wealth, possessions, success, even family and friends. Only in these things can our separated self hope to construct a soft landing, though of course it is a fool's paradise. Understandably, our separated self is shocked and disappointed with God.

Notice how our connected self points us to the inner life for safety and salvation. Jesus and his first followers all point us to the inner life of relationships not to our outer life. Nothing can separate us from the love of God in Christ Jesus, (Rom 8:38-39). Rejoice always, for the Lord is near, don't worry about anything, (Phil. 4:4-7). Remember, I am always with you, (Matt. 28:20). Our hope is entirely in our relationship with God, not in the ups and downs of our life's circumstances.

Some Last Thoughts

Now having heard our choices, let's make our decision: Which voice will we follow today? Our separated self or our connected self? Will we be disappointed with God? Or, will we rest safely in God's arms? "Nothing can separate us from the love of Christ Jesus...Nothing!" – Romans 8. Hold on to that thought today.

Be slow to judge anything in our life as bad.
Be unwavering in our view that Christ is in everything,
Especially our darkest hour.

DAY 22

··

Dare to Be Vulnerable

If we seek deep friendships,
We need to be more open with each other,
And at times, even vulnerable.

Introduction

Jesus told his friends, "unless you change and become like children, you will never enter the kingdom of heaven," (Matthew 18:3). An important trait of little children is their willingness to be vulnerable. They are role models for us as we have conversations with our inner life. Today, let's consider the importance of being vulnerable.

Some Observations to Ponder:

By nature, we are slow to let people know us, really know us. We keep our true selves hidden, probably for good reason. But if we are going to develop real friendships, we need to be more open, and at times, even vulnerable.

There is a curious thing about what we share with others. Talking about our successes puts up a wall, driving people away. Talking about our failures tears down some of those walls that keep us separated and lonely. We create just a little opening for people to get to know us, really know us. It is the same with our conversations with God.

Jesus spoke about his failures and humiliations. He spoke of what awaited him: a cross, not a crown. He openly wept when his people rejected his love. He was discouraged that his friends didn't get what he was doing. He was saddened that his friends fell asleep just when he needed them most.

Does this vulnerability surprise us? Do we wonder, "What manner of teacher, king, God is so open and vulnerable?" Does this openness make us think less of him as our teacher or king, even as our friend? Maybe. But as our friend, his vulnerability invites us to come closer.

The Stories that Shape Us

For the last three years, as the days get shorter in the fall and the darkness outside my office windows comes earlier and earlier, I notice a change comes over me. I sense a darkness in my heart. Everywhere I turn, there it is. Nothing has changed from earlier in the day. I don't understand any of the triggers for this inner darkness. Except the shortening of daylight outside. I don't know how to adequately describe it except to say, "I am lonely."

For several weeks, in my conversations with my inner life, I noted this darkness of my heart, this loneliness. Then one day out of nowhere, I seemed to sense that Jesus not only understood my loneliness but also may even feel this same loneliness. This was new to me, a strange thought for me.

Could it be true that Christ so identifies with us that he experiences all of our deepest feelings, even our loneliness? Could it be that Christ knows all that we suffer, not as an outsider looking in, but as one who has been there himself? I don't know. But as I imagined this possibility, I sensed a shared vulnerability that is part of all deep friendships. In the days that followed, in our conversations, Christ and I unpacked loneliness. Our relationship took a deep dive into what it meant to be friends.

A Few Practices to Try:

Spend time with little children. Notice their vulnerability. When they are sad, they cry. When they are happy, they laugh. How might you become just a little more like them? Notice how challenging this is for our separated self. Do we find any encouragement from our connected self? Listen carefully to our inner voices.

Spend some time with Christ, seeking nothing from him. Just observing him, soaking up the wisdom of his presence. Notice his vulnerability? If Christ is vulnerable, maybe we can be vulnerable, too? If we are lonely, tired, despised, hated, lost, tell him. See what happens.

Some Last Thoughts

My loneliness has been reframed. It is like the church bells of the great cathedrals on Christmas Eve, announcing, "Christ is born, in my heart, this day!" It is like that phone call late at night, from a friend asking, "Can we talk?" To which, I answer, "Of course."

It might be lonelier without the Loneliness.
– Emily Dickenson

DAY 23

What to Do with the Troubling Stuff?

You have to keep breaking your
heart until it opens.
-- Rumi

Introduction

Take a beach ball and push it under the water. Pushing it deeper and deeper, finally it pops out, unexpectedly, with great force and usually sideways. That's what happens to the troubling stuff of life if we push it out of sight. Sooner or later, it builds up such force that it demands to be taken seriously, maybe popping us in the nose. Better to take the beach ball out of the water earlier than to be "hit in the nose" later. Today, let's consider what to do with the troubling stuff we find in our inner life.

Some Observations to Ponder:

As we pay attention to our inner life, we uncover some troubling stuff: regret, grief, fears, worries…thoughts of being unworthy or unloved. This is our separated self talking. Hearing the voice of our separated self, we decide that the inner life is too scary! We stay away from our thoughts, our feelings, even from our God.

Christ taught us to make friends with the troubling stuff. Bring it closer. "If any want to become my followers, let them deny themselves and take up their cross and follow me," (Matthew 16:24). To "take up our cross" is to make friends with the troubling stuff of our lives. And when we face the things that trouble us, we learn to fall into the loving arms of God, our soft landing. This is the connected self talking. What a comforting voice it is!

The Stories that Shape Us

"It is Well With My Soul," is one of my favorite hymns. The lyrics are written by Horatio G. Spafford who knew something about life's bumpy ride. He was a successful attorney and real estate investor who lost a fortune in the great Chicago fire of 1871. Around the same time, his beloved four-year-old son died of scarlet fever.

Thinking a vacation would do his family some good, he sent his wife and four daughters on a ship to England, planning to join them after he finished some pressing business at home. However, while crossing the Atlantic Ocean, the ship was involved in a terrible collision and sunk. More than 200 people lost their lives, including all four of Horatio Spafford's precious daughters. His wife, Anna, survived the tragedy. Arriving in England, she sent a telegram to her husband that began: "Saved alone. What shall I do?"

Horatio immediately set sail for England. At one point during his voyage, the captain of the ship, aware of the tragedy that had struck the Spafford family, summoned Horatio to tell him that they were now passing over the spot where the shipwreck had occurred. As Horatio thought about his daughters, words of comfort and hope filled his heart and mind. He wrote them down, and they have since become a well-loved hymn:

> When peace like a river, attendeth my way,
> When sorrows like sea billows roll—
> Whatever my lot, thou hast taught me to know
> It is well, it is well with my soul.

The separated self, using only the tool of human reason, will never comprehend the comfort and hope of these words. The connected self does not comprehend them either, but on a deeper level knows that they are true. The experience of God's loving presence in our worst bumpy ride is that peace that passes all understanding, (Philippians 4). This experience is our soft landing.

A Few Practices to Try:

What is troubling us today? Notice how our separated self magnifies it, making it so bad, we just want to run away and hide, or pretend it's not there. Notice how our connected self invites us to be brave. Face these challenges. Christ promises to be with us in life, especially in the tough stuff. Pay attention to our inner voices today. Which voice will we follow? This is the main practice of friends of Jesus. "Face the tough stuff."

Name one troubling thing we could face today. Can we do just one little thing to bring this troubling thing out into the open? Naming it is a start. Noting our thoughts or feelings or wants also is a good step. We don't have to solve this troubling thing. Just be present to it and notice that Christ is present as well. I wonder what we and Christ will come up with to help us face this powerful force of that "beach ball pushed below the surface."

For all those "beach balls" we've pushed beneath the surface, out of sight, out of mind, Christ is our soft landing.

Some Last Thoughts

St. Paul discovered that when he admitted his own weakness and powerlessness, his heart then opened to God's strength. "When I am weak in myself (Paul wrote), I find a comforting strength in God." Horatio Spafford also experienced this truth.

The wound is where the light comes in.

— Rumi

DAY 24

··

What to Do with the Pleasant Stuff?

A child's Christmas joy:
Wrapping paper hiding splendid gifts? Or,
Splendid gifts hiding a parent's love?

Introduction

Today, let's consider the pleasant things of life. No problem, we
think. That's what we like and live for — the pleasant things of
life. But they too may need special attention in our inner life.

Some Observations to Ponder:

As we pay attention to our life, we find many things to our liking:
our body, our health, our family and friends, our ability to make
a difference in the world. Life is so sweet. But sooner or later, all
of the really nice things in life are taken from us. If we've built
our hope for a soft landing on these, what will we do?

This is a really tricky thing for us to get. We understand that
building a life based on fear and scarcity won't work. But what
about the really sweet things of life?

The challenge is to be conscious of the hope these sweet things
bring. They are not the Giver of life and joy, they are gifts pointing

us to the Giver. An important distinction to keep in mind. One that our two voices are always arguing about.

The Stories that Shape Us

As I look back over the last three years of my diagnosis of cancer. I am struck by how my heart has changed. The first months of the diagnosis were dark days. We had no idea how long I had to live. But in the three years I've been given, my health has remained stable, maybe gotten some better.

Because of this cancer diagnosis, I am living a truth that has transformed me. "My life doesn't belong to me." My days are quite literally in the hands of God. My life has a flow about it that is exciting. At night, I can't wait to fall asleep and then to wake up and see what God and I will do tomorrow. This is true in my relationships with others, in my writing, and my cello playing. I am very happy.

But here is the tricky thing for me. All these experiences that bring so much hope and joy to my life, they are temporary. Sooner or later, I will die. They will not help or comfort me then. Have I merely exchanged one external comfort for another?

I'm learning to see that my hopes for a soft landing are still too much attached to conversations with my separated self. Like a little child at Christmas, I see too much the toys, and not enough the love behind them. I need to develop the view of my connected self, a more subtle watching of the inner life, my hopes and dreams, my feelings and thoughts, how they all point me to the one who alone is my soft landing.

A Few Practices to Try

First, learn to give thanks for all the good things in our life. Live a life of gratitude.

Secondly, notice how our separated self attaches hope to all of the good things of life. Be mindful, the good things won't give us that soft landing, but they do point us to the One who can.

Finally, learn to look with the eyes of the connected self. See our loving God behind all the good things of life. "Look through" the sweet things of life, until our focus lets go of them, and rests contentedly in the presence of our loving God.

Some Last Thoughts

As we age, the really nice things we like are slowly taken from us. We have less that grabs our attention that we may have more space in our hearts for loving God. At first this can be troublesome until we understand the plan: "Less things, more God."

> The pleasant things in life are merely the
> finger pointing at the moon.

DAY 25

Gratitude

If the only prayer you said was thank
you, that would be enough.
– Meister Eckhart

Introduction

Gratitude is a simple but effective spiritual practice for so much of
life's bumpy ride. Today, let's consider the importance of gratitude.

Some Observations to Ponder

Children see life through the lens of fairy tales. Bad things happen
when a wicked witch casts a spell on us. As grown ups, we let
go of the stories about witches and spells, but we still experience
something akin to "spells." We can easily be overtaken by anger,
fear, worry, jealousy, or greed. Where is the prince, the son of the
king, who comes to rescue us?

The Stories that Shape Us

Once upon a time, there was a king and queen who irritated a
wicked fairy. To get back at them, the fairy put a curse on the little
princess of the king and queen, announcing that she will die on
her sixteenth birthday when she pricks her finger on a spinning
wheel. As the princess's sixteenth birthday approached, some

good fairies altered the evil fairies curse by putting the princess into a deep sleep from which she could only awaken by a kiss of a prince. Now, there's a lot of drama as this story gets played out. But in the end, the prince found the young woman, now called "Sleeping Beauty," and he kissed her. She awakened and so too all of her kingdom awakened from a similar slumber. And they all live happily ever after.

So what's the point of this fairy tale? I see how we can so easily come under the influence of strong negative feelings and thoughts that just don't go away. They are like magical spells. Wouldn't it be nice to have some prince kiss us and awaken us to a much better life? That prince sounds a lot like Christ, the son of our Heavenly King, and Father. "To kiss" him, or be kissed by him, suggests a loving, life changing encounter with Christ. It hints at the imagery of Christ as the groom and we are the bride.

I think gratitude is that kiss, that one thing that connects us to God and breaks any spell of strong emotions or thoughts that just won't go away. If you recognise Christ near you, loving you, are there really any strong negative emotions that you need to harbor? Are there any thoughts that you need to keep ruminating over? Gratitude to God, for anything, breaks the spell that has come upon us.

A Few Practices to Try

When we are under the spell of any dark emotion, try gratitude. Gratitude is a powerful spell breaker. Gratitude for anything — for warm socks, for our bed, for a sunrise. Gratitude can instantly move us out of the domain of our separated self. Like magic, the anger, fear, sadness, and all other spells are gone. Gratitude is the golden door into the presence of our connected self.

Some Last Thoughts

Imagine Christ with us, right now. Truly present to us. But of course, this is not just "our imagination" — Christ IS here! When we are truly present to Christ, fully knowing his loving presence, do we really need to fear anything? Or, be greedy? Or any of the rest?

> When I started counting my blessings,
> my whole life turned around.
> – Willie Nelson

DAY 26

Remember the Poor

Spending time with the poor is spending time with Christ. How sweet it is!

Introduction

We are surrounded by the poor, people who from the world's point of view are living lives of disadvantage. We may decide to offer them some help. But do we ever think that they might have some gift to offer us? Today, let's consider the importance of remembering the poor.

Some Observations to Ponder:

At certain times of the year, we are encouraged to "remember the poor." See the Salvation Army bell ringer outside the shopping mall each December. We have so much, many have so little. We can spare some pocket change. Maybe more.

Jesus was attracted to the poor, the disadvantaged, the outcasts. They were ready for his message. Long ago, they had stopped being under the influence of the separated self. Jesus noted that they entered the inner life before the rich and powerful. They are truly Jesus' first followers. What do they know that we don't?

The Stories that Shape Us

I heard this story on public radio, on a program about money matters. I don't know if the details are correct but I know that the story is true.

A successful businessman took a vacation to a small island in the Caribbean. While there, each morning at sunrise a fisherman took his little boat and went fishing. Around 11 am he returned with some fish. He could have caught more had he fished all day.

After watching the fisherman for several days, the businessman finally asked him, "I see you come in early each with only a few fish. Why don't you stay out the whole day." The fisherman was surprised by the question. His schedule for each day seemed so obvious to him. He replied, "I come in at 11 to unload my catch so that I can eat lunch with my family, then I enjoy a nice siesta with my wife, and then we go into town where we meet our friends to sing and dance into the night."

Now it was the business man's turn to be surprised. "Wait a minute. Look what you could do. Fish for a whole day, soon you can get a second boat and hire a worker, in time you can have a whole fleet of boats, then in time you can build a cannery here and ship your fish throughout the United States, and finally in time, and this is the really good part, you can move to New York City to manage your empire, shipping your fish all over the world."

Quietly reflecting on this advice, the fisherman finally replied, "But when would I have time for a siesta each afternoon with my wife and when would I be able to sing and dance the night away with my friends?"

"Oh, that's the beauty of my plan," the businessman eagerly continued, "in maybe thirty years of working really hard you can come down here for a two week vacation each year. Then you can fish in the morning, take an afternoon siesta with your wife, and sing and dance the night away with your friends"

A Few Practices to Try:

Spend time with the poor, those who are disadvantaged, the outcasts of life. They have a wisdom that our separated self cannot comprehend. But it speaks to our connected self with a simple elegance. Beneath their various forms of poverty that shout at us, listen carefully for their whispered wisdom to spend time with first the inner life, to seek first the kingdom of God.

Summary

Can we take advice from the disadvantaged, the poor, the physically challenged, the people overlooked by our culture. They are often Christ's "first followers." We give them a few spare coins. They give us treasures that no thief can break in and steal from us.

> When would I have time for a siesta
> each afternoon with my wife?
> When would I be able to sing and dance
> the night away with friends?

DAY 27

Holding a Baby

For all the things my hands have held the best by far is you.

Introduction

Today, let's consider babies. They have little status, no power to make things happen either for themselves or for us. Yet, God once came to us as a little baby, calling our attention to these magnificent, insignificant ones.

Some Observations to Ponder:

Take a look at the babies in our life. How have we related to them in the past? We gently rock them, calming the child, and ourselves, as well. We hold the baby close, kissing the child's head, we both feel loved.

We hold the baby, and in a way, the baby holds us.

The Stories that Shape Us

Recently, my wife and I have welcomed into our family our fifth grandchild. What a sweetheart. Each grandchild is so precious to us. As parents, the birth of our children was such a happy day. Holding them and watching them grow up right before our eyes was so sweet. But looking back on that time with our own children, I realize that I couldn't give them the same kind of attention that I now give my grandkids. As parents, we had so many things to do: make a living to support the kids, keep up the house, help the kids establish their own boundaries, and, depending on the day, spend a little or a lot of time saying, "No!" As grandparents we have just one job: to keep pouring more and more love into their little hearts. Their parents are doing just fine with all the rest.

I find myself returning home from time spent with my grandkids, face beaming with a smile, heart about to explode with love. What a joy to talk to the older grandkids. They are so smart and caring, eager to be loved and to give love. And they laugh at grandpa's jokes. Wonderful!

And those little babies, to hold them, to have them reach out their hands to me as if to say, "Pick me up!" As I snuggle with them, I experience love at a very deep level. My heart is so full of love.

A Few Practices to Try:

Imagine holding Jesus in our arms as that little babe of Bethlehem. Watch carefully what we do with him? See how we love him, simply love him. Be present to each other in love. Notice how we stop living in the past or future. Notice how we find a sense of calm, love, and of being connected.

The image of holding God as a baby moves us out of our heads into our hearts. This is heaven, isn't it?

Some Last Thoughts

Little wonder that Christ first came to us as a baby. How might we imagine our time with Christ? Think of Mary holding the

Christchild. No words. Just this deep inner experience. What is that experience like for us?

> There are places in the heart you don't even
> know exist until you love a child.
> – Anne Lamott

DAY 28

Choose the Life We Have

Ten years from now, make sure you can say, You chose your life. You didn't settle for it.
— Mandy Hale

Introduction

Are we spending our energies and resources, each day fighting against the life we have been given? "What if we act as if the life we have is the life we would have chosen?"

Some Observations to Ponder

Life is challenging: Health issues, financial problems, grief and loss. As time goes by, the challenges become more challenging. We fight against the life we have. It's a losing battle. How long can we keep resisting our life with its ups and downs?

Read again, with beginner's eyes, the stories of the Bible. See how some people choose to be victims while others choose the life that they were given. When Jesus speaks about taking up our cross and following him (Matthew 16:24), he's not asking us to be victims but instead, he's really talking about choosing the life that we have. The cross is that part of our lives that we don't want, don't like, or don't understand. But, we pick it up, we choose it as part of our following Christ. By letting go of our hopes and dreams, we can open our hearts to following Jesus down paths we don't know, don't understand, or wouldn't have chosen on our own. We become followers of Christ.

The Stories that Shape Us

As a little child, I had a very strong attraction to the story of Joseph in the Old Testament. (Genesis 37-50). You may remember the story. Joseph angered his older brothers with his dreams of greatness. In a moment of deep resentment over their father's obvious love for Joseph, they sold him into slavery. That began many years of suffering as he missed the love of his father and as he lived first as a slave and then as a prisoner.

What struck me as a child was how Joseph always gave life a good face. In whatever horrible situation he found himself, he knew God was with him. He chose the life he was given. While in prison, he offered his administrative skills to the head jailer.

From all outward appearances, it seemed like God had forgotten Joseph. But after decades of slavery and imprisonment, God brought Joseph out of prison and made him the second most powerful man in Egypt. At the end of his life, he understood the path God had for him. He told his brothers, "even though you intended to do harm to me, God intended it for good, in order to preserve a numerous people, as he is doing today," (Genesis 50:20).

Joseph chose the life he was given. Contrast this with the Old Testament prophet Jonah who definitely did not choose the life given him. Read his story. God called Jonah to give Nineveh a message. He refused and ran the other way. See how Jonah fought his life. God still used him. But Jonah got no joy from it. How sad.

A Few Practices to Try

First, observe the events and people in our life. See how we label them. Some we call good, some we call bad. But how do we really know?

Secondly, notice that this labeling isn't our voice, it's our separated self.

Thirdly, hold on to the "bad" things. Wait and see. Watch. God is in these, too. Watch. Consider past evaluations of bad things in our life. Did they all turn out bad?

Finally, after a time, see if there is some gift for us in this "bad" thing?

Some Last Thoughts

Today, the choice is ours: to be like Joseph or Jonah, to listen to the voice of our connected self or our separated self.

> Even though you intended to do harm to
> me, God intended it for good.
> Genesis 50:20

DAY 29

Laughter

There are many ways to the Divine.
I have chosen the way of song, dance, and laughter.
– Rumi

Introduction

Laughter is not always welcomed by religious or spiritual people. Life is too serious for any laughter. Or, is it the other way around? Life is too important to take seriously?

Some Observations to Ponder

Laughter is such an easy thing to do, even babies smile and laugh. What do they know that we don't?

Some laughter flows from our pain, hurting others or ourselves. This is not the laughter of the conscious inner life.

We have been taught to see our world in all seriousness. In a thousand ways we have been conditioned to think: laughter is inappropriate. This is the voice of our separated self. This is our life in the outer world.

Attending a wedding banquet, in the presence of the bride and groom, it is not laughter that is inappropriate but a sour disposition.

Story

A college professor of mine walked around the campus with a permanent smile on his face. Really more of a grin than a smile. All of us freshmen noticed it. When we were alone, we asked, "What's up with him?"

I can't remember ever seeing him without a smile. On one occasion, we were in the midst of a blizzard. Ice crystals, like little knives, struck our faces as we walked across the campus. It was brutal. No one was happy about having to be out in that weather. But there was our professor walking by us with the usual big smile on his face. He looked as if he were strolling on a beach in Hawaii. What a character!

One day, a few of us students got up the nerve to ask him about this smile. He good naturedly answered our question, and yes, he was smiling. He said to us, "In Philippians 4, Paul tells us to rejoice in the Lord always, for the Lord is near. I'm just doing what Paul has taught. I'm rejoicing." "Oh," we all thought to ourselves. "Well, now we know and it makes a little sense. Why the sour look on our faces if the resurrected Christ is by our side? He had a point."

Smiling was a powerful spiritual practice for one of the most popular profs on campus. I believe that there was this flywheel action going on between his outer practice of smiling and his inner condition of experiencing that soft landing. His outward practice of smiling encouraged his inner condition of feeling safe in the Lord's care. And his inner condition of feeling safe encouraged his outward condition of smiling.

A Few Practices to Try

Notice today how our separated self sees everything as "Life and death." Serious stuff. Poor thing. He is all alone in this big, scary world.

But this need not be our response to life. Let our smile reflect Christ's presence. Choose our connected self. Choose laughter. Christ is with us!

So for today, "see" Christ really with us. What is the look on our face?

Some Last Thoughts

Whether we wear a frown or a smile is a decision we make. It reflects what's happening with the conversation between our separated self and our connected self. Decide which one you'll follow today. And then smile, laugh heartily, you are in good hands.

> I have many problems. My lips don't
> know that. They always smile.
> – Charlie Chaplin

DAY 30

Be Our Own Easter

Whatever is true, whatever is honorable, whatever is just,
Whatever is pure, whatever is pleasing,
whatever is commendable,
If there is any excellence and if there is
anything worthy of praise,
Think about these things.
Philippians 4:8

Introduction

Easter is a wonderful celebration: the music, the people, the flowers, and above all else, the message — "Christ is risen, alleluia!" What if every day were Easter?

Some Observations to Ponder

The joy of Easter soon fades away. We return to our lives with all of the cares, worries and frustrations. Sometimes this return to normal takes a week or two, but usually just a few days, and often, just a few hours.

For the friends of Jesus, the joy of that first Easter seemed to stay with them. It remained with them as they continued to see Jesus in their midst. He showed up among them for 40 days. And after he ascended into heaven, he promised to show up through the

Holy Spirit. The Spirit was given to them, and to us, this constant companion to comfort us.

In the story of the two disciples from Emmaus, walking home after that first Easter, we learn to experience Jesus' loving presence in the Bible. After the resurrected Christ leaves them, they observe, "Were not our hearts burning within us while he was talking to us on the road, while he was opening the scriptures to us?" (Luke 24:32).

The Stories that Shape Us

The first morning after receiving my cancer diagnosis, I had a hard time getting out of bed. I had such a heavy weight resting on my heart. I had no idea what to do. I felt hopeless. I was dying and nothing could change that. Then from deep inside of me, I sensed a voice say to me, "Get up. Go for your morning walk as you always do." So I did. I had no other plan. I walked my usual path and listened to those two inner voices.

As expected, my separated self had a lot of fears to unpack. It would take months to unpack them all. In fact, there remains something to unpack even today, but now less to do with that initial shock of the cancer diagnosis. Now I need to unpack the daily stuff that troubles my separated self. There is always something.

From the first day, I also have listened to my connected self. For some years before this, I had memorized my own "Go To" list of songs, wise sayings, psalms and Bible passages. That first day, I turned to my "Go To" list and found a better voice to follow than my separated self. I had the strength to face the day. My cancer was still with me. But so was Christ. I had the courage to face the day. But just that day. I needed to return again the next day and repeat this process. This is now my practice each day, my path to that soft landing after a bumpy ride.

A Few Practices to Try

Put together a "Go To" list of Bible passages that bring hope, joy, calm, and encouragement for the journey. A few recommendations. (Add to the list.)

> Psalm 23:1, The Lord is my shepherd.
> Psalm 121:7, The Lord will keep you from all evil.
> Romans 8:38-39, Nothing can separate you from God's love.
> Philippians 4:4-7, Rejoice! because the Lord is near
> Colossians 3:3-4, For you have died, and your life is hidden with Christ in God.

I also include poetry, songs and hymns, some short sayings, like the ones found at the beginning and ending of each Day in this book.

Memorize them. Remember them. Begin your day with them. Let your connected self speak to you and fill you with God's presence.

Some Last Thoughts

We begin our day processing the separated self's fears. But then, we can add to that mix the comforting words of our connected self, we can think about the words of our "Go To" list. We can choose to live in the joy and hope of Easter every day. "Christ is risen, alleluia!"

> Do whatever best awakens you to love.
> — Teresa of Avila

DAY 31

···

Walking into the Light

Ours is not a caravan of despair,
Come, even if you have broken your vows a thousand times.
Come, yet again, come, come.
– Rumi

Introduction

There are some common experiences that happen to us as we age especially as we consider the prospects of our own deaths. As we get closer to the Light of God's presence, the darkness of our own hearts becomes clearer to us and more of a bother. Today, let's talk about what happens as we grow old. We are walking into the Light.

Some Observations to Ponder

There seems to be a need for an extra measure of love as we age.

There are unique challenges of the spiritual journey as we pass through different stages. In our youth, our separated self chatters away about our bodies — preoccupation with food, misunderstandings about our sexuality, struggles with sloth, or an undue focus on our body image. In our middle age, our separated self shifts the conversation more to worldly matters -– pride, possessions, or our position at work and in the world.

Then, as we come into old age, as our minds diminish and our bodies weaken, we think we are at last "home free." No more inner struggles. We are surprised by the separated self's shift to spiritual conversations. The separated self just won't let go of our past, reminding us of all the hurtful things we have done. This can be a lonely time if we only have one voice speaking to us — the separated self.

The Stories that Shape Us

As a young pastor in my mid twenties, I monthly met with Al, an army veteran, confined to a wheelchair and housebound. After several months of building up trust, he finally shared with me what was haunting him. "Pastor, I killed men in the war. Can God forgive me?" Without giving it much thought, I answered, "Of course." But the question did not go away. In between our visits, his separated self kept taking him back to the war.

For many months, he asked the same question, "Can God forgive me." I kept giving him the same answer, "Of course." After a while, I stopped trying to answer the question. I was only keeping the conversation going with his separated self. So I turned the main focus of our conversation to his connected self. We talked about God's love. I think his question would always be with him in the background, sometimes more pressing than at other times. But he learned to listen also to his connected self, to lean into God's grace and love.

The question about forgiveness was the hole into his soul that could only be filled with the love of God's presence. The more he opened up to his need for God's love, the more that love poured into his heart.

A Few Practices to Try

As we grow old, we notice how our separated self shames us with our past mistakes. He keeps us away from God. Notice whose voice is speaking to us and who's got the problem? Us? No. God? No. Our separated self? Bingo!

If we stop listening to our separated self, stop the fear and shame, he loses us. So our separated self has a vested interest in going over past mistakes again and again. It keeps us away from God. This energy to "capture us" once and for all increases as it appears that soon we will be totally out of the separated self's grasp.

Notice how our connected self sees us now, clothed in God's love, washed clean. Smile, laugh, come into the banquet. All is now ready.

These practices suggested here are summed up quite nicely in Jesus' advice to us, "Take up your cross and follow me," (Matthew 16:24). Or, as we are learning to frame things: Note our separated self's complaints and then follow our connected self. You have a choice.

Some Last Thoughts

Once we come to midlife, we notice little hints that we are walking into the light of God's presence. In that light, we see more of our own darkness. But do not fear, God washes all that away in abundant love. Stay close today to your connected self.

> We are all children coming inside from recess
> with varying degrees of dirt on us.
> — Shannon L. Alder

DAY 32

Decluttering

People may spend their whole lives
climbing the ladder of success
Only to find, once they reach the top, the
ladder is leaning against the wrong wall.
– Thomas Merton.

Introduction

Decluttering was a popular buzzword a few years ago. We were invited to look at our homes and get rid of all the things that were no longer bringing us joy. Decluttering would allow us to live more simply and be more in touch with ourselves. Many found some truth in this. The same truth seems to apply to our spiritual journey. Are there things we can now let go of?

Some Observations to Ponder

Notice how our interests in life evolve. What caught our eye as little children, lost its sparkle as we became teens. And our passions as young adults changed as we moved into our middle ages. There is this natural progression as we age regarding what we think may give us that abundant life.

When I was a child, I remember a song sung by Peggy Lee, "Is That All There Is?" The lyrics walk us through this parade of things that capture our hearts, but only for a while. Then, as we get to the end of our lives, we may run out of sparkly things to chase after and then we say with a growing sadness, "Is that all there is?" That may be the question for many in our culture today.

The Stories that Shape Us

About halfway through my career as a pastor, I was given good advice about decluttering my work. In the early years of being a pastor, I was told to try a lot of different kinds of ministries: work with youth and adults; try a small congregation and then a large one; serve as a solo pastor, an assistant pastor, and also a senior pastor. But then, when I reached about 45 years of age, I was told to narrow down my focus. Give my best and fullest attention to two or three aspects of being a pastor, be a specialist rather than a generalist. This plan worked well for me. I became the senior pastor of a large church with a large staff. This gave me the opportunity to spend my time looking at the big picture while others on the staff took very good care of those important details of ministry. I loved this narrow vision of my work as a pastor. Without a doubt, this was the best time in my work as a pastor.

For the last two decades, I've found myself doing the same with my personal interests in life. I was decluttering before I had even heard the word. I once was an avid fisherman, hunter, and I ran a few marathons. But then, I just seemed to lose interest in them. Gardening and landscaping, too. And now with the diagnosis of stage 4 cancer, I find each day precious and not to be wasted. Most of life has lost its sparkle. I'm just not interested. I sometimes wonder if I am depressed. But then, I see the joy I have each morning as I arise and get on with my day. Sometimes, I'm so excited to begin my day, I awake at 3 am ready to go. I try to stay in bed until 4:30 am. But some days, I just can't contain myself. I have never been so happy.

My life has decluttered down to just a few things: people in my life — my wife, my family, my friends, and fellow travelers I meet along the way; my art — my cello and my writing; and above all else, my Lord — each day as I go for my morning walk, I ask, "And what shall we do today?"

Life has become deliciously sweet. Especially any time I can just hang out with God.

A Few Practices to Try

What in life right now no longer gives us joy or a sense of hope? Can we let go of that?

What are the things that interest us now? How can we make more time for them?

As our mind and body age, as we have less on our mind, and as we have less energy to do things, what encouragement can we find for sitting together with God on our front porch and just enjoying the company?

Some Last Thoughts

As we get older, if we listen to our mind and bodies, there is so much that we can't do anymore. Our separated self grieves these losses. Not so our connected self. More time for relationships. More time for God. More time to love.

> What do you need to do? Pack your bags,
> Go to the station without them, Catch the train,
> And leave yourself behind.
> – Wei Wu Wei

DAY 33

....

Imagination

How else would God speak to me if
not through my imagination?
— Joan of Arc

Introduction

The imagination is a playground for children, not the setting for
serious thoughts about God. Or, is it? Let's consider the place of
our imagination in our inner journey.

Some Observations to Ponder:

The imagination is not just for kids, adults use it, too. How
often in life are we asked to use our imagination? We're told
to "imagine being a teacher or nurse, or retiring early?" Our
imagination "sees" outside the box we have placed our life in.
Our imagination also creates space for love, beauty, forgiveness,
and God.

Joan of Arc, while on trial, was accused of using her imagination:
"All of your messages from God are just from your imagination."

"Yes," she admitted, "How else would God speak to me if not
through my imagination?"

How else indeed. Our mind is far too small for the things of God. We must use our imagination to get there.

"Is not the imagination a dangerous place for us?" Yes, the separated self's imagination that flows from fear is dangerous. No, the connected self's imagination that flows from compassion is not dangerous, it's utterly necessary. Start imagining, "seeing," all the people in our life who need our compassionate presence.

The Stories that Shape Us

When I was in my mid-forties, I noticed that my personal spirituality had become a bit dry. I was good at going through all the motions of being a somewhat adequate pastor. I knew most of the right words to say. I got the "dance" people expected of me. But on the inside, I felt empty. I began a three year course on spiritual direction. I was intrigued by the books of women and men who had deep personal experiences of God.

The course on becoming a spiritual director[2] was my first intentional experience with the inner life that we've been talking about these 40 days. To become a spiritual director, I needed to be in spiritual direction myself, something new for me.

I met monthly with my spiritual director. We quickly got to the heart of the matter. She asked me, "How do you go about listening to God?" Well, I really didn't have an answer. That's the reason that I came to her for spiritual direction.

"I don't," I answered.

---

[2] I use the name spiritual director because most people seem to understand it. I prefer the title of "Soul Friend" as found in the Celtic tradition. It feels less authoritarian and more of a peer relationship, it more closely follows my new calling, "We're all just walking each other home," (Ram Dass).

She said, "Well, why don't you try just imagining what God might say to you?" But nothing came. Then, she said, well, "Why don't you imagine that you are God. What would you say to yourself?" Again, nothing. Then she said, "Well, then, imagine a friend speaking to you? What might they ask? How might they respond to your questions and answers?"

Bingo. That worked for me. I could imagine people, living and dead, people I knew and others I didn't, historical and Biblical people. My inner conversations got very rich. It was only a small jump to imagining God as part of this choir singing their sweet melody to my heart.

A Few Practices to Try

As we begin our day, imagine Christ with us in everything we do. Learn to "see" Christ. As we get busy with our day, it's easy to lose sight of that presence. When that happens, gently return to his promise: "remember, I am with you always," (Matthew 28:20).

After we have become accustomed to this practice, enter the imagination again. This time imagine a conversation with Christ. Pose a question and wait for an answer. Over the years, as I practice this and suggest it for others, the most valuable and reusable question to pose to Christ is this, "Well, Lord, what shall we do today?" I have found answers to this question not in the agenda of my separated self, but in the events of my life, the opportunities placed before me to act with compassion and abundance for a world in need of these. And at the end of the day, ask that follow up question, "And how was today, Lord? How'd we do?"

Listen to Christ speak to us in the thoughts that just come into our mind, or the words and needs of our neighbor, or the longing of our heart to do good things for others.

In time, we more easily recognize the inner voice of our separated self who comes to us with words of fear and scarcity. And we also learn to recognize our connected self voice who comes to us with compassion and abundance.

There comes a time of listening to our connected self that simply amazes us. Our thoughts and words and actions are just not like us. They are so gracious and caring. "Who is this person?" we ask ourselves. But of course, it isn't us, at least not the us of our old separated self. It is our connected self. That "Aha" moment of recognizing the inner dwelling of God's Spirit in us is life changing.

Some Last Thoughts

We need to live in our imagination:

> To show compassion or offer forgiveness to unlovable people,
> To practice Christ's constant presence and ongoing conversation,
> To laugh and smile even through the challenging times,
> To find that soft landing in the midst of a bumpy ride.

Some say, "Believe in God."
I say, "Imagine God here with us."
They are both the same.

DAY 34

The Ten Black Beans

Stress is the trash of modern life — we all generate it,
But if you don't dispose of it properly,
It will pile up and overtake your life.
— Danzae Pace

Introduction

I like to watch mysteries on Public Television, particularly those
that have interesting character development. The solving of the
mystery is secondary to my keen interest in how characters evolve,
grow into relationships, and just plain figure out how life works.

The Stories that Shape Us

Today, let's change our routine and begin with a story from the
PBS TV series, "Astrid,"[3] who has unique gifts for solving murder
mysteries: highly sensitive to her surroundings and a photographic
memory.

Astrid's high sensitivity has its challenges. She is stressed by loud
noises, large crowds, and new situations. On one occasion, during
a particularly stressful time for her, a friend placed 10 black beans
into her outstretched hand. In silence she quizzically stared at the
beans. Finally she asked, "What are these?'

---

[3] Public Television, "Astride," Season 2, Episode 4.

Astrid's friend had known her for a long time. He understood that life could be overwhelming for her. Occasionally life was so overwhelming, it required hospitalization. But he said none of that to her. He just said, "You look tired."

She replied, "I am. I'm working on a murder case, I don't get much sleep at night."

"I thought as much," he replied. He continued, "Place the black beans in your right pocket. Move one bean to your left pocket when something stresses you or makes you nervous or tires you. Stressful things like noise and crowds. But even good things like working at a job you like. Don't let all the beans move into your left pocket. Watch how your day is going. If the beans in your right pocket become few, do something to move beans back to your right pocket."

She thought for a moment. Then she smiled, and without saying a word, she just walked away. This was her custom when confronted with new information. Her friend said to himself, "She got it."

Some Observations to Ponder:

I can relate to Asride. For me, life has occasionally been quite stressful. I've had my moments of stomach aches as a little child, and then migraines much of my adult life. My body was telling me that I'm overwhelmed. I wish that someone would have given me my 10 black beans.

I think two good things would have come from having my own 10 black beans. First, I would have been more conscious of my inner life, particularly the pain caused by my separated self. For most of my life, I was quite unconscious of this pain, only my body knew and carried it. Secondly, I might have much, much earlier explored ways to move the black beans back from my left pocket back into my right pocket.

A Few Practices to Try:

Carrying around 10 black beans may seem like a real bother. But, carrying around, in an unconscious way, the pain from our separated self can be an even bigger bother. So when might we move beans from our right pocket to our left pocket? There are all sorts of measuring tools on the internet for this. One that I like is called, "The Life Change Index Scale." Check it out. It gives a point value to various stresses, such as:

- Death of a spouse is 100
- Retirement is 45
- New family member is 39
- Change schools is 20
- Vacation is 13
- Christmas approaching is 12

The list is much more comprehensive. But it helps us to develop our own set of stressors. What stresses you? What reduces your stress? We are probably all too familiar with what stresses us. But what can we do to relieve stress in a healthy way? Early in my ministry, I discovered that spiritual practices, like worship, prayer, or Bible study, no longer refreshed my tired heart as they once did. They had become tools of my trade, no longer that safe landing for my inner life. I realized that my hour walk each morning is an important way for me to move my beans back to my right pocket.

We all need to personalize this process of what it is that moves the black beans out of our right hand pocket and then moves them back again.

Some Last Thoughts

Right now, in which pocket are your 10 black beans? What do you need to do?

> In times of stress, the first thing I do is go back to basics ...
> Am I eating right, am I getting enough sleep,
> Am I getting some physical and mental exercise every day?
> — Edward Albert

DAY 35

··

Amazing Love:
The Contemplative Path

"Even darkness must pass. A new day will come.
And when the sun shines it will shine out the clearer.
Those were the stories that stayed with
you, that meant something,
Even if you were too small to understand why."
— Sam Gamgee encouraging Frodo
in "The Lord of the Rings"

"Life must be lived looking forward,
But it can only be understood looking backward."
— Soren Kierkegaard.

Introduction

Grace, the amazing grace of God, was a formative teaching and
practice of my early spiritual life. When I reached midlife, amazing
grace gave way to amazing love. In my moment of greatest need,
the diagnosis of cancer, I turned to love, not to grace.

Some Observations to Ponder:

"Amazing Grace" is a hymn that comforts us as we look to our
past. We often sing it at funerals. Grace frames our life in a simple

storyline that can loop endlessly: "We sin, we say that we are sorry, and God forgives us. Repeat. Repeat. Repeat." But what about our future, the new life calling out to us?

Love may be a more fertile place to grow into our calling as joyful children of God. Grace tells us our past is okay, love tells us our present and future are wonderful. All healthy relationships experience grace, but as they deepen, grace seems to fade into the background and love becomes all in all.

The Stories that Shape Us

When I first heard the news that I had stage 4 cancer, my mind shut down. I felt so lost. I could see no path ahead. But now, after three years, I realize that I was on a path that I had been pursuing for the past three decades. I just didn't have a name for it until now. I once was on a path of grace, but then in midlife I moved over to a path of love.

For the first forty years of my life, I followed a path of grace: "I sin, I confess my sins, God forgives me. Repeat, repeat, repeat." This path served me well until midlife when I had sufficiently dealt with that angry God of my childhood and no longer found as much life or energy in grace. So I explored God's amazing love. I developed a friendship with God. I came closer to this loving God. This is what I did for the next thirty years.

Fast forward to the diagnosis of cancer at age 68. I didn't feel God's anger so I didn't fall into God's grace. Instead I fell into God's love, what I now call "Job's path," though I didn't realize it at the time:

- Like Job, in one moment, my whole life fell apart.
- Like Job, I was in this cloud of unknowing. I didn't understand.

- Like Job, I did not turn to grace just to get my old life back.
- Like Job, I didn't say, "I'm sorry, God. Can I have a 'do over'?"
- Like Job, I held on to my sufferings.
- Like Job, I was painfully conscious.
- Like Job, I held onto this loving God not knowing why.
- And finally, like Job, I was transformed by God's love.

A Few Practices to Try:

Where have we experienced a love so wonderful, unconditional and extravagant? What was that like? How has that love changed us?

Imagine God loving us in this same way, but even more so. Amazing love. Say these words: "I am loved by God." Repeat them again and again throughout the day. Feel God's hand holding our hand. Feel God's arms around us, holding us close. Literally experience that amazing love.

Some Last Thoughts

Grace is indeed amazing when we encounter that angry God of our separated self. There is no other way to find relief. But love is exponentially amazing when we encounter the loving God of our connected self. Amazing Love!

Stay present to life until it changes
you – amazing love.

DAY 36

· ·

Saved and Safe

Once you become fearless, life becomes limitless.
– Lisa Lieberman-Wang

For you have died, and your life is hidden with Christ in God.
When Christ who is your life is revealed,
Then you also will be revealed with him in glory.
Colossians 3:3-4

Introduction

There is value in our spirituality, the practice of our faith, not just
for when we die, but for how we live right now. Today let's talk
about not only being saved, but also being safe.

Some Observations to Ponder:

For much of the 20th century, and for many centuries before that,
being saved was it. Going to heaven when we die was the main focus
of the church. Saved but not safe. As the 20th century came to a close,
some people leaned into God's love rather than God's anger. And if
God so loves the whole world, then shouldn't we feel safe? Very safe?

What exactly is safe now? The hope that our little dreams all
come true? Probably not. Our relationship to God who will never
abandon us, in life or death? Yes. That's it!

The Stories that Shape Us

I really like the HBO mini series, "Band of Brothers." It is the story of a group of American soldiers, heroes from World War II. They were members of Easy Company of the 101ˢᵗ Airborne Division of the U.S. Army. It's a realistic portrayal of the battles they fought from D-Day to the end of the war.

In one scene, Easy Company was to pass along orders to a group of American soldiers pinned down by the enemy. So the men ran across an open field. But when the bullets started flying, their captain froze in fear, slumping down in the middle of that open field. His men did the same. They were all in danger of being shot, one at a time. The captain's superior officer yelled at the captain to get up and cross the field. But the captain wouldn't move. So the officer looked at another captain and ordered him, "Get out there and move those men across the field."

Now that's when the story gets interesting. Without a moment's hesitation, he ran out on the field with bullets flying all around him. He came to the frightened captain and ordered him to move on. But he wouldn't. So the replacement captain jumped up and ran across the rest of the field, right into the middle of German soldiers who were so surprised by his brazen actions that they stopped shooting and just stared at him. He passed through the enemy soldiers, ran to where the American soldiers were hiding behind a barrier, he jumped over the barrier and gave the message to the stranded soldiers. Then, having done his work, he jumped back over the barrier, ran through the camp of the enemy soldiers a second time, back across that open field and returned to where he started.

Later, one of his soldiers asked, "Weren't you afraid of dying?" He replied, "To do this work, you must think of yourself as already dead." He ended the war without any injuries.

A Few Practices to Try:

"Think of ourselves as already dead." I know. That's a really morbid thought. But it can free us from the worries of our separated self. It can keep us in the present which is such a gift.

Some Last Thoughts

"You must think of yourself as already dead." How many of our fears, tears, worries, regrets and all the rest vanish when we just die to this life of the small self. Having died to our separated self, we find it easy to follow our Lord wherever he may lead.

Let's just finally die to our separated self,
All of its hopes and dreams, fears and worries,
So we can live to our connected self
And the love of God that will keep us safe.

DAY 37

After the Crisis

God is our refuge and strength, a very present help in trouble.
Therefore we will not fear, though the earth should change,
Though the mountains shake in the heart of the sea;
Though its waters roar and foam.
Psalm 46:1-3

Introduction

There are two moments when our separated self is particularly
troublesome: when we are in the middle of a crisis and when we
have gotten through it. The second moment may be more subtle,
but it is just as bothersome.

Some Observations to Ponder:

The Bible is filled with stories of people in crisis. St. John of the
cross, a sixteenth century poet and mystic, called this time of
crisis "the dark night of the soul." It is that moment when God
seems to have abandoned us. The sweetness of life with God is
suddenly gone.

Job's story in the Bible is primarily this crisis of the soul. But he
is not alone. Jacob suffers when he returns home after 20 years,
wondering if his brother still wants to kill him (Genesis 33).
The disciples in that storm tossed boat question Jesus, "Teacher,

do you not care that we are perishing?" (Mark 4:38). Peter suffers after he denies knowing Christ the night before Christ's death (Luke 22:62). David in Psalm 22 describes this moment of crisis, "My God, my God, why have you forsaken me?" And, of course, Christ quotes from Psalm 22 to describe his soul's own crisis while on the cross dying – he too felt abandoned by God (Matthew 27:46).

I find Noah's story of this soul crisis of particular interest. He seemed to do well with the crisis of the flood, but the suffering that comes to him after the flood drives him to excessive drinking (Genesis 9:21). So, too, with all of us, it is not just the crisis of the moment that challenges us, but also the repercussions that follow when the storm has passed.

The Stories that Shape Us

Cancer has been my dark night of the soul. Everything was turned upside down. Nothing was left for me to hang on to, for comfort, for laughter, for hope. And then, things got better. I assumed that there would be no more dark nights. I was wrong.

About three years into cancer, my wife and I experienced that all too common event: our computer was hacked into. We were in full crisis mode: trying to rebuild the walls of security that kept our private matters and our finances away from the bad guys. And all the time kicking ourselves for letting these bad actors into our computer and our lives. I was too busy to notice my separated self. I was in a full blown "manage the storm" mode.

In time, we felt that we had weathered the storm. Things calmed down, life returned to normal. But then, I noticed that my separated self was having trouble. Like someone being seasick in a boat might feel woozy for a few hours or even days after getting off the boat, my separated self was definitely suffering the after effects of all that had happened. I started waking up in the middle of the night worried about my grandchildren. Nothing was wrong with them. But even the slightest possibility of danger for them, in my sleep, was magnified into a real danger, needing immediate action on my part. I would awake at 2 am and not be able to sleep.

Only when I recognized the voice of my hurting separated self, could I begin to shrink down all of these fears and address them with my connected self. In my daily walk, I needed to have this conversation with those two inner voices. And then, throughout the day, return to the decision of my watcher: "Be still and know that I am God," (Psalm 46:10).

A Few Practices to Try:

Consider the chatter of our separated self when we were in the midst of a soul crisis, when we felt that God had abandoned us. What was that like? How did we get through that crisis? Did we turn to our connected self to help us? How long did we wait?

Consider after the crisis was over. When the storm had passed and everything was calm again. Was there still some uneasiness that we couldn't quite put our finger on? Were we hypervigilant about dangers that might happen? Learn to look for that voice after a crisis, expect that voice, and then bring the connected self into the discussion?

Some Last Thoughts

Watch for the fears of our separated self, not just in the time of crisis but after the crisis when things have calmed down. That can be the moment when we are most unconscious of, and thus most vulnerable to, the stress we still carry. Be the watcher.

Be still, and know that I am God.
Psalm 46:10

DAY 38

··

Expectations

He was swimming in a sea of other people's expectations.
Men had drowned in seas like that.
— Robert Jordan

Introduction

Unmet expectations can be a source of great discomfort in our
inner life. Let's explore how our expectations play into our inner
conversations and our bumpy ride.

Some Observations to Ponder:

Expectations seem to be a natural by-product of being a member of
our culture. Everywhere we turn, we run into expectations from
ourselves, our boss, our family, our neighbors, our government,
our church, and our world. And maybe worst of all, from God.
We are constantly thinking about expectations as a way to evaluate
our strategies, measure our level of success, and even establish our
worth. Expectations belong to the world of our separated self.

Our world stresses expectations as really important. But too often,
the outcome of our plans, or of our lives, is really beyond our
control. Stressing expectations in our outer life often brings great
stress to us in our inner life.

The Stories that Shape Us

Early in my work as a pastor, I followed the leadership style of older pastors. I considered the issue before us, devised a plan, in prayer asked God to bless our plan, and then worked really hard to make it happen. That "worked really hard" part was driven by expectations, mine and other people's, maybe even God's, too. I had a lot riding on this: my reputation as a competent pastor, my self-worth as a person. Expectations stressed me. I found myself often locked into **BEV** (**B**itterness, **E**ntitlement, and being a **V**ictim) – all thanks to conversations in my inner life with my separated self.

I found my life got incredibly more enjoyable when I let go of some of my expectations and focused instead on the process of working with God. I left the outcome with God. I pointed the congregation in a certain direction. But I led with an openness about outcomes: "I could be wrong. But let's try this and see." Sometimes I was wrong. Sometimes God had a very different plan, a better plan. We weren't stressed out about expectations. We all just stayed close to God. We watched what God was doing in our midst.

This joy of letting go of expectations is doubly true for my expectations of others. There have been moments, due to my own high expectations for myself, I got stressed out by others who weren't living up to my expectations. That wasn't any fun for me. It wasn't fun for them. But when I let go of my expectations of people and just loved them, they started living into being the people of God that I had always hoped they might be.

A Few Practices to Try:

Emphasizing the process over the end result, removes the stress and makes for such an enjoyable life. Learn to enjoy the "doing" with

God over any expectations set beforehand. Pay attention to what God's doing, join God, don't think so much about expectations.

As we begin our day, we do need to have some vision for where we are going and what we might do today. But is there a place where we can give up just a little control over planning for the day? When asked what we are doing today, can we say to ourselves and to others, "I'm not sure. I'm looking forward to at least one surprise where I see God working and then I jump right in and join God. Just one surprise today!"

Some Last Thoughts

Invited by our connected self to live in abundant love with ourselves and others, let go of expectations. Be prepared to be surprised by what love can accomplish!

> Know that everything is in perfect order,
> Whether you understand it or not.
> — Valery Satterwhite

DAY 39

....

Welcome Our Separated Self

No visitor arrives without a gift
And no guest leaves without a blessing.
– John O'Donohue

Introduction

We've now spent 39 days together, watching for all the sneaky ways our separated self can make an entrance in our lives. Today we pose the question, "Is there anything good that comes from the separated self?

Some Observations to Ponder:

If the separated self is such a challenge to live with, why not just get rid of it? Our appetite can cause some pain if we haven't eaten for a while, or can cause us a different kind of pain if we don't know when to stop eating. But we don't get rid of our appetite. We appreciate the gift that our appetite brings to us. It reminds us to eat. So we keep it around. So, too, our separated self has value in our inner life.

Our separated self is the canary in the mineshaft, it screams, "Something is wrong!" "There's fear, anxiety, loneliness, and hopelessness abroad in our life." But when our separated self also offers us a solution to the fears that it sees, then that isn't helpful.

Like a fire alarm, our separated self can't offer any solutions for our fears, it simply gets our attention. And that's a good thing, both for fire alarms and for our separated self.

The Stories that Shape Us

I love the story of St. Francis "kissing the leper." Perhaps it is more fiction than fact, but there is an inner truth about the story, both for Francis and for us.

Before Francis heard God's call to follow, he lived a rich and pampered life of a wealthy young man. One night, dressed in his finest, he set off on horseback for a night of partying with friends. Traveling along a narrow path, he met a leper blocking his way. He had always been particularly repulsed by lepers, their smell and deformities disgusted him. He tried to steer around the leper but it was no use. Finally, he was forced to dismount from his horse and moved the leper off the path. As he touched the leper's arm, something happened inside Francis' heart. No words could ever explain to Francis what happened that night. It made no sense at all to him. But in the blink of an eye, he no longer was repulsed by the smell of rotting flesh. He leaned closer and kissed the leper. He was never the same again. In that kiss, God's compassion for him and for all people became a life changing reality for him.

For all of his life, up until that moment, up until that kiss, lepers repulsed Francis. But in the kiss of the leper, Francis was overwhelmed with divine love. He would forever see lepers and all the other hurting people of the world as God's gifts to him. In these, the least of all people, his inner life was flooded with God's love. From that moment on, he gave himself to the world, to the poor and needy, and to lepers.

A Few Practices to Try

Sit with our separated self's fears and all the other strong emotions connected to those fears. Sit with the anger, the worries, the shame, the guilt, the loneliness, and all the rest. At first, we create a little distance from our separated self and all of these fears. This is helpful to establish the identity of our connected self. But after a while, we need to rethink our response to the separated self. It tells us some truth about our inner life, a truth that we possibly have been avoiding. What fears, anger, worries, guilt, loneliness are we ignoring right now?

There is a part of us that has not yet been converted to our connected self. We need to bring God's love into every nook and cranny of our bodies, into every compartment of our hearts, into every thought of our minds. This is a big project. Where do we start? Start with where the fearful voice of our separated self points. One at a time we bring compassion and God's presence into our entire life.

Some Last Thoughts

In the same way that Francis changed his mind about lepers, we might also see our separated self as one who has so much to teach us about compassion. Like Francis, we complete our conversion to love by loving our separated self.

Keep our connected self close and our separated self even closer.

DAY 40

··

God's Last Word

Prayer is not overcoming God's reluctance.
It is laying hold of God's willingness.
– Julian of Norwich

Introduction

Today is our 40th and last "Conversation Starter." I am filled with
doubts. "Have I forgotten something really important to share with
you?" Quite likely, I have. But I find great consolation in offering
to you Julian of Norwich as the focus of our last day. I invite you
into imagining a lifelong ongoing conversation with her that will
carry you through every bump along the way. Her message is one
of love: God is love, eternal love. God can only be who God is.
There is no condemnation, only acceptance. Julian's message is as
needed today as it was in her day in 14th century England.

Some Observations to Ponder:

Julian was a woman of contrasts and contradictions, often at odds
with just about everything in her culture.

1. She was a woman and a great teacher in the church,
   unusual for her time as well as for much of history.
2. She was one of the most famous theologians and mystics of all
   time, yet we know practically nothing about her personal life.

3. She lived in a time of great turmoil: Her church was struggling with two different popes simultaneously claiming to be God's final voice on earth, the people were suffering the consequences of a long drawn-out war between England and France, and for 21 years of her life, England suffered the first wave of bubonic plague. She had much to be pessimistic about. And yet, her message was one great optimism in the abiding love of God.

4. Julian consistently depicts Jesus as a compassionate guide who listens patiently without judgment, consistent with the figure in the Bible but not so much with the Christ figure of her day who was only too often portrayed by the church as encouraging all manner of violence, death and destruction.

5. In the midst of such a fearful world, she believed in a friendly universe. Only an immediate experience of the loving God could convince her of this truth.

The Stories that Shape Us

Julian of Norwich lived from 1342 until about 1430. In May 1373, she experienced an illness that all, including Julian herself, thought would be her death. But she was healed. In the midst of that near death experience, she received 16 visions from God that took the rest of her life to unpack. For 20 years, she was an anchoress in the church of St. Julian in Norwich, England, from which we have given her a name.

In those days, an anchoress was a hermit who lived in the midst of a community rather than off by herself in some deserted place. Julian stood at the center of her faith community as an anchor for many who were blown here and there by the storms of life. Julian lived in a cell connected to St. Julian's church where she had three windows: one into the church where she could join worship and receive the sacrament, one to the outside where a servant could supply her physical needs, and one for the many people who came for spiritual advice. She spent years in her cell, praying, advising, encouraging all who came to her to see God as love. She was that anchor for her generation and now for our generation today.

To all who came to her for advice, no matter what the particulars might have been, she ended with the same comforting words, the same words she offers us today:

> But all shall be well,
> And all shall be well.
> All manner of things shall be well.

A Few Practices to Try:

Imagine coming to Julian's cell in the great church of St. Julian in Norwich. What might you say to her? What troubles weigh on your heart today? What might she say to you?

Remember Julian's words: Jesus is mother, companion, advisor, defender, and savior, always present and available to help but never judgmental or bullying. God is as close as a mother's love and gentle as the best of friends. Unpack each word Julian used to describe Jesus, one at a time, bring it into conversations with Julian and with God? How does each rich word open up new avenues of hope and joy?

See Julian personify our connected self. See Julian's world personify our separated self

Some Last Thoughts

The words of Julian of Norwich are the words of one who has passed into and through life's most challenging challenges. She has found her loving Lord, who is gently holding all of history. There is nothing to fear. There is nothing more to say.

"And all shall be well."

+   +   +

Not unto us, O Lord, not unto us,
But to thy name give the glory.[4]

---

[4] From the Latin hymn: *Non nobis, Domine, non nobis, Sed nomini tuo da gloriam.*

APPENDIX I

THE THREE INNER VOICES OF GALATIANS 2:20,
"IT IS NO LONGER I WHO LIVE, BUT
CHRIST WHO LIVES IN ME."

In Galatians 2:20, I find a brief but elegant description of the three inner voices I have come to know and appreciate in my journey with cancer.

In Paul's words, "I who no longer live," I find **the separated self**. This is an earlier self that still shows up in our lives, often at the most inopportune times, to stir up all sorts of fears, causing us much suffering and innumerable problems. I am separated from myself, from those I love, from other people, from nature, and especially, from God.

In the story of Adam and Eve's "Fall" from God's favor (Genesis 3), they experienced this separation in all of its painful facets. They are separated from God when they must leave their home with God in paradise. They are separated from nature when they are told that nature will no longer willingly give of itself to support them. They will earn their food by the sweat of their brows. They are separated from each other as Adam blames Eve for this mess. And finally, they are separated from their own inner lives as they hide from God, experiencing guilt and fear for what they have done, as well as shame due to their nakedness. The remainder of Genesis is the extended story of the separated self taking over our narrative.

The separated self is the voice of scarcity and fear. The core problem isn't one of morality or sin, that is merely the tip of the iceberg. The real issues are discovered below the surface, in the inner life of heart and mind, (Matthew 15:19-21).

The separated self is an earlier voice in our lives. A voice with which we once completely identified. We thought the voice to be our own. But now, in our reconnection to God, we can create some distance from that first voice. But, quite unexpectedly, and especially in moments of HALT (i. E., when we are experiencing hunger, anger, loneliness or tiredness), we easily slide back into that voice, thinking of it as our own. Whenever we are living in scarcity or fear, whenever we are not fully present, we are living in our separated self.

In Paul's words, "the Christ who lives in me," I find **the connected self**. This is that new self Jesus speaks of when he talks about being "born again," (John 3:3-4), or, when Jesus speaks of a friendship with God so intimate that we are connected to God at a very deep level. So Jesus says, "I am the vine and you are the branch, whoever dwells in me and I in him bears much fruit," (John 15:1-11). This is the voice of abundance and compassion.

We seem to have little problem hearing the first voice of the separated self. We have lived with it so long, we hear it everywhere – that voice of fear and scarcity. But the second voice is quieter, less demanding of our attention. Of course, we hear this voice in the Bible. But this voice, once we recognize it as the voice of love, is also found everywhere. We see it in our world, whether it is the Northern Lights or a rose, whether in a baby's laugh or a lover's embrace, whether in favorite poetry, songs, stories, or in the wisdom of various spiritual traditions.

I find the third voice in Paul's words, "in me." In this third voice, we see ourselves as **the watcher**. We observe the first two voices, noticing what they say to us and how they interact with each other. They have some rather heated arguments. This is good. It's what keeps us from "limping along" all day or even our entire life, not knowing if we should go this way or that way. The watcher makes a decision about which voice to follow. It is a powerful thing to make that decision, to have an undivided heart and mind, with a heart on fire for the Lord to go about your day.

Printed in the United States
by Baker & Taylor Publisher Services